TEN HOUSES

TEN HOUSES

Edited by Oscar Riera Ojeda

Ace Architects

First published in the United States of America by:

Rockport Publishers Inc.

33 Commercial Street

Gloucester, Massachusetts 01930

Telephone: 978-282-9590

Fax: 978-283-2742

www.rockpub.com

Other distribution by

Rockport Publishers Inc.

ISBN 1-56496-491-4

10 9 8 7 6 5 4 3 2 1

Printed in China

Cover Photograph: Jordan Residence. Photograph by Alan Weintraub

Back Cover Photographs are of projects on pages (from left to right, top to bottom) 12, 24, 34, 44, 58, 70, 82, 98, 110, 116 Page 2: Allen Residence. Photograph by Alan Weintraub

Contents

6 Foreword by Elaine Louie

8 Introduction by David Bonetti

Selected Works

12 Telegraph Hill Houses, San Francisco, California

24 Querio Residence, Oakland, California

34 Rancho Diablo, Lafayette, California

44 Tabancay/Austin Residence, Berkeley, California

58 Jordan Residence, Oakland, California

70 Allen Residence, Oakland, California

82 House on Twin Peaks, San Francisco, California

98 Roth Residence, Oakland, California

110 Saravia Residence, Tegucigalpa, Honduras

116 Six Houses, Oakland, California

122 Selected Buildings and Projects

123 Firm Profile

124 Photographic Credits

Foreword

by Elaine Louie

When Ace Architects designs a building, they incorporate what could be called the "Ahh" factor. When people first see an Ace building—the Arabian Nights fantasy in Berkeley with the copper-colored dome, or the Jordan residence in Oakland, which looks like a miniaturization of Bernard Maybeck's Hearst Hall complete with pointed Gothic arch shape—their first reaction is usually a gasp of breath, a quick intake, an "Ahh."

Their office, which is close by the San Francisco Bay, resembles a sea monster with a beak-like face, its head a dome covered with copper scales. A client's house in San Francisco was designed to resemble a barn with an adjacent silo enclosing a circular staircase. Why leave a staircase plain, when it can be painted in gold Dutch leaf, so that it gleams and swirls, and resembles the inside of a nautilus chamber? Why leave something ordinary when it can be made extraordinary?

"We consider ourselves the opposite of minimalist," said Lucia Howard, who with David Weingarten is principal of Ace Architects in Oakland, California. The desire to be maximalists originated more than twenty years ago, when they met at the University of California at Berkeley, where both were graduate students in architecture. "Our teachers and classmates thought architecture to be a serious, abstract, gray-and-white endeavor," Ms. Howard said. But she and Mr. Weingarten did not.

She wrote her thesis on "content" in architecture, how architecture can tell a story, how it can have overt and hidden symbolism, and how it can embody historical references and personal fantasies. Mr. Weingarten wrote his thesis on "color," how in the world things are colorful, and how buildings, too, ought to be colorful. "That's a prejudice," he said, "not a reasoned position. It's not a dialectic, simply an observation." Since no one else agreed with them, they formed Ace Architects.

For the Arabian Nights house in Berkeley, the architects didn't just incorporate the Arabian dome, but also designed turrets and balconies, round rooms and square. The furniture could not be banal, so they designed an octagonal table with Moorish-patterned etched glass to recline around, and surrounded it with pillows in vermilion, emerald, and ochre silk brocades. For the house with the gold circular stairway, they designed a bathroom of glass mosaics in shades of blue—ice blue, turquoise, robin's egg, cobalt—and scattered an occasional tiny gold tile amid the blue. The bathroom resembles an underwater grotto, whose colors shift and fade like the colors of water. And every now and then, there is the glitter of gold, like a fragment of buried treasure.

In an Ace Architects house, contrary to Mies' dictum, it isn't God that lurks in every detail. But it might be wit.

Elaine Louie writes on both design and food. She lives in Manhattan.

Left: Topper Residence, Mill Valley, California. **Opposite Page:** Kenny/Reichard Residence, San Francisco, California.

ntroduction

by David Bonetti

Above: *Tunnel Road Castle, Oakland, California.*

Of the three characteristics of architecture that Vitruvius identified—firmness, commodity, and delight—Ace Architects comes down most decidedly in favor of delight. Perhaps the greatest damage the modern movement inflicted on architecture was its tacit prohibition of humor, whimsy, and personal expression of a kind that falls over into wretched but delightful excess. The great hope that many had for postmodernism was that, under its more inclusive and tolerant tent, the delicious frivolity of certain strains of traditional architecture might make a comeback. We all love Rome's Hertziana Library. Why can't we build such a whimsical project today?

Most postmodernist decoration unfortunately turned out to be as joyless as modernist austerity. It was just more vulgar. It also pointed up most contemporary designers' lack of imagination. Having studied under Mies or Walter Gropius or one of their followers, they had had any tendency toward imagination stomped out of them. For every Robert Venturi or Charles Moore, there were a thousand Michael Graves wannabes, exploring the most arcane reaches of Egyptian revival, without having the least understanding of (or real interest in) the original.

Ace Architects hasn't as yet produced a revived Egyptian as far as I know, but it did create an Arabian Nights fantasy for a Berkeley client who relished his Saturday matinees at the movies watching Sinbad. Edward Said might not be amused, but if he were to speak with the charmingly and infectiously loopy Ace principals David Weingarten and Lucia Howard, he might share with them his own fantasy, which they might help him realize in built form. They did, after all, produce a house with twin saxophone-like towers for a jazz amateur. I might not like having to look at the so-called Saxophone House, myself, but it just demonstrates that everyone's most personal fantasies do not occupy equal positions on the good-taste scale.

The Ace house I would most like to move into and make my own is the Telegraph Hill House, one Ace designed for Weingarten himself. Like him, I am a history buff, a lover of architectural styles past and present, and that house neatly recapitulates—in a particularly witty way—the three codified periods of what's been called the Bay Area tradition of domestic architecture.

1985

On the façade, which rises steeply over a pedestrian lane, the two major local traditions are grafted together in what amounts to a stylistic shotgun wedding. The generously arched entry recalls the turn-of-the-century arts-and-crafts eclecticism of Bernard Maybeck, Willis Polk, and Julia Morgan. Emerging at a jaunty angle is a three-story element with the straightforward lack of nonsense typical of mid-century Bay Area modernist William Wurster, in which Weingarten even dared to be as boring as his source. Inside, the madness shifts into third gear, and somehow, in homage to Charles Moore, Weingarten managed to appropriate Sir John Soane for the Bay Area.

What roots Ace in solid ground and serves to rein in some of its more over-the-top tendencies is its profound knowledge and serious appreciation of architectural history. The Telegraph Hill House is not the only one of its houses historically informed—although it might go farthest in what the firm calls an archeology of Bay Area styles. That Arabian Nights fantasy in Berkeley, for instance, boasts a procession of spaces down a set of steps that are reminiscent of the sequences of public spaces in several classic Maybeck houses.

Maybeck frequently is Ace's touchstone. The small-scale Jordan Residence, a replacement for a house lost in the 1991 Oakland Hills fire, is boldly based on Maybeck's 1899 magniloquent Hearst Hall, itself neatly burnt, for lovers of symmetry, in a 1922 fire. Ace has a reputation for creating wacky, "fun" buildings. When Ace presented its first thoughts on this house to the client, she complained that the house wasn't "fun" enough. So, Ace went back to the drawing boards and came up with a house that abounds in "fun." Vitruvius would be delighted.

The Jordan Residence is exuberant in its modesty. (Ace gives you a lot of bang for the buck.) It fills its tight lot to the max, but its narrow frontage allows only two-thirds of Hearst Hall to be appropriated. Where Maybeck was symmetrical, Ace is asymmetrical. Where Maybeck's pile squarely hugs the ground, Ace's form rises with a narrow Rapunzel-like tower. The interior is dominated by a great room rising to a peak with neo-Gothic wooden arches, and it comes complete with a balcony just waiting for a band of roving troubadours.

Ace's penchant for historical referencing comes to one peak with a sextet of speculative houses in the Oakland Hills, in which the history of California style— mission, Monterey colonial, Victorian, art deco, modern, and deconstructivist— will be reprised in six easy lessons. For all their outward differences, however, the interiors will be identical. Ace has proposed using the same floor plan, flipping it three times for symmetry. Call it façadism if you will, but say it with a smile.

While other architectural firms struggle to define and refine a signature style, Ace remains open to all stylistic possibilities. (It has even, in the Allen Residence, adapted International style to its own purposes.) The key to its open-mindedness, I think, lies in its own delight in play and toys. Indeed, Weingarten might be better known as a collector of miniature souvenir buildings than as an architect. (The collection he and Margaret Majua have assembled is the subject of a delightful 1996 Abrams book, *Souvenir Buildings, Miniature Monuments*.) In addition to houses, Ace designs commercial buildings and urban design projects; it is entirely appropriate that among recent commercial projects the firm has designed a store for refrigerator magnets at Disney World.

It's often been observed that creativity flourishes in children and dries up slowly but surely with maturity. Those who have held on to their creativity have kept the child within them alive. With its toys, Ace Architects nourishes its childlike side. In its celebration of the miniature, the toy, the symbolic object, it is not alone among design firms. Charles Moore, Weingarten's uncle, was a collector of objects variously magical and ordinary, and that great California design team composed of Charles and Ray Eames found constant delight and creative renewal in the rare, strange, and banal objects they filled their home and office with. Their examples suggest that enthusiasm for play leads to the best solutions.

David Bonetti is the art critic for the San Francisco Examiner.

Above Right: Bank of America Home Loan Campaign Posters. *Middle and Below:* Architecturals Miniatures in the "Building Building." *Opposite Page Top and Center:* Blumenfeld Residence, Berkeley, California. *Below: Tabancay/Austin Residence, Berkeley,* California.

No importa cómo lo uses, puedes **ahorrar dinero** con cualquiera de nuestros préstamos hipotecarios.

Con tasas de interès y cargos reducidos.

No matter what kind of house you want, you can **save money** with a BofA mortgage.

As little as 3% down. Ask us how.

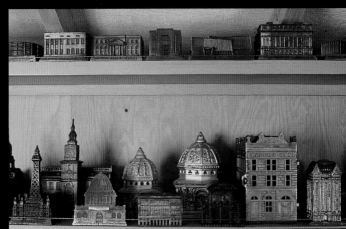

Telegraph Hill Houses

San Francisco, California

Unlike other architectural modes, the Bay Region style—whose presence was first suggested in 1948 by the critic Lewis Mumford—to this day resists formal definition. Instead, it is often described as an architectural attitude—casual, not pretentious, though sophisticated; reveling in cheap, often local, materials; alluding, sometimes grandly, to historically and geographically distant, occasionally fictive, places; and embracing life out-of-doors.

Some of the greatest and most characteristic Bay Region style buildings—Maybeck's Christian Science Church, Wurster's Gregory Farmhouse, Moore, Lyndon, Turnbull, and Whitaker's Sea Ranch—share many of these traits, even as they were fully contemporary works. These, and other signature Bay Region style buildings, also almost always employ elements of other styles-Gothic's pointed arch, Classicism's decorative language, even the swirling lines of Baroque—the better to attach current interests to other places and times.

If in the nineteenth century eclecticism was often the default approach to architectural design, for much of the twentieth century it was something of a dirty word. Modernist Mumford's interest in the Bay Region style did not, of course, extend to its eclecticism.

This building, on the other hand, housing two apartments on the eastern slope of Telegraph Hill, set among some of the oldest houses in San Francisco, is fully eclectic. While employing the Bay Region style's attitude towards materials, allusion, and the out-of-doors, it also reconstitutes some of its memorable forms.

The narrow (22.5 feet/7 meters wide) site faces a much narrower pedestrian lane and is inaccessible to vehicles. Toward this lane, the building appears a fanciful reconstruction of a place made up over time, assembled of pieces from the history of the Bay Region style, beginning in the late nineteenth century. Toward San Francisco Bay, the architecture rises like the cities of Troy—a newer story built atop an older story, topped by still another layer.

This approach includes the building's interior, where the lower apartment is gotten up in early Bay Region's classicizing dress, while the upper apartment sports its international style and, later, vernacular and aedicular refinements.

Near the end of the twentieth century, with design a global business, there is attention yet again to regionalism, critical and otherwise, in American architecture. One irony attending this is that architecture in the Bay Area, whose stylistic history extends a hundred years, is increasingly turned out nearly every way but in the Bay Region style.

This building, by contrast, roots for the home team, for the constructive possibilities of the regional idiom in all its variety, and for the allusive continuities of this architectural style with an attitude.

West Elevation   1. WURSTER AT HOME 2. MOORE AS THE MOON 3. RUINED BUST OF MAYBECK

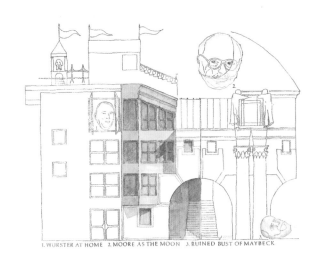

East Elevation   c. 1887   1946   1970

Left: *Fireplace, lifted from Egyptian-styled chimney-pieces in Piranesi's Diverse Maniere, is festooned with Mexican Day of the Dead figures, petrified logs, and a stone gargoyle. The glass hearth allows firelight to flicker in the rooms below.*

Opposite Page: *The houses front and back on Darrell Place, a narrow pedestrian lane on Telegraph Hill.*

Right: *The silver- and blue-finished walls of the elliptically planned foyer, viewed from the diminutive Architecture Room.*

Opposite Page Above: *Mirror-backed niche in the Architecture Room.* **Below:** *Painted plaster figures of Sculpture and Architecture flank stairs to the foyer.*

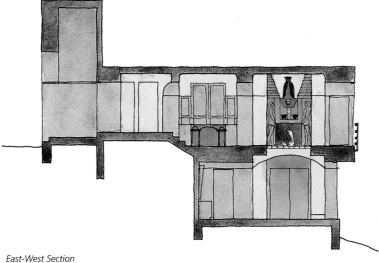

East-West Section

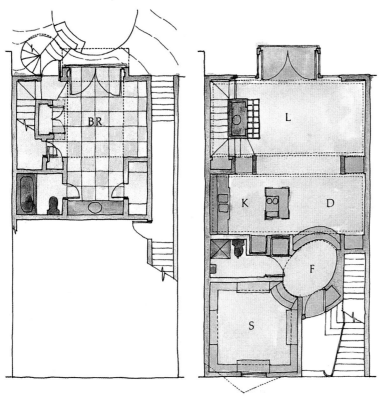

First Level

Second Level

Left: *Yellow-hued Architecture Room is a ten-foot (three-meter) cube. Ceiling mural pictures the several periods of the Bay Region Style.*

Opposite Page Above: *Ceramic tile walls at guest bath.* **Below:** *Seashell-shaped basin.*

Right: The figure of Sculpture, poised at the foyer steps, considers the kitchen beyond.

Opposite Page Above: Kitchen island, a miniature of the room which houses it, is fashioned from stainless steel. **Below:** Vertical grain redwood walls provide a setting for stained plywood table and chairs, inspired by Piranesi's furniture designs for Cardinal Rezzonico.

Following Spread Left: Living and dining of the upper, more Modern Bay Region-styled house. **Right:** Double-height living space looks towards Yerba Buena Island.

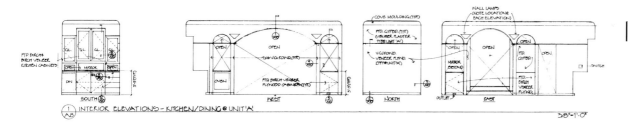

PTD. BIRCH
BIRCH VENEER
KITCHEN CABINETS

OPEN | MIRROR | OPEN

DIN

SOUTH

OPEN | OPEN

WEST

COVE MOULDING (TYP)

PTD. GYPBD.(TYP)
(VENEER PLASTER
(TYP) UNIT 'A')

V.G. RDND.
VENEER PLYWD.
(TYP) UNIT'A')

PTD. BIRCH VENEER
PLYWD. (CABINET TYPE)

NORTH

WALL LAMPS
(NOTE LOCATION
EACH ELEVATION)

OPEN | OPEN | OPEN

OPEN

MIRROR
BEYOND

PTD.
GYPBD

PTD.
BIRCH
VENEER
PLYWD

OUTLET   EAST   SWITCH

①
A8   INTERIOR ELEVATIONS - KITCHEN/DINING @ UNIT 'A'   3/8"=1'-0"

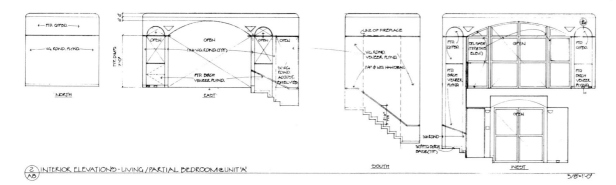

PTD. GYPBD.

V.G. RDND. PLYWD.

NORTH

OPEN | OPEN | OPEN

1X6 V.G. RDND (TYP)

PTD. BIRCH
VENEER PLYWD.

EAST

1X V.G.
RDND. ADJUST.
SHELVES

LINE OF FIREPLACE

V.G. RDND.
VENEER PLYWD.

1 1/4" Ø WD. HANDRAIL

V.G. RDND.

PTD. BIRCH
BASE (TYP)

SOUTH

PTD.
GYPBD

GYP. BACK
(TYP IN THIS
ELEV.)

OPEN

PTD.
GYPBD

PTD.
BIRCH
VENEER
PLYWD

PTD.
BIRCH
VENEER
PLYWD

OPEN

WEST

②
A8   INTERIOR ELEVATIONS - LIVING/PARTIAL BEDROOM @ UNIT 'A'   3/8"=1'-0"

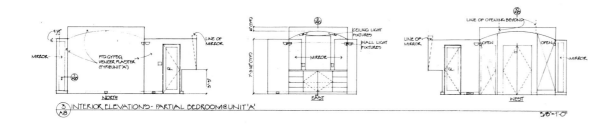

MIRROR

PTD. GYPBD.
VENEER PLASTER
(TYP UNIT 'A')

LINE OF
MIRROR

NORTH

CEILING LIGHT
FIXTURES

MIRROR

WALL LIGHT
FIXTURES

EAST

LINE OF OPENING BEYOND

LINE OF
MIRROR

OPEN   OPEN

MIRROR

WEST

③
A8   INTERIOR ELEVATIONS - PARTIAL BEDROOM @ UNIT 'A'   3/8"=1'-0"

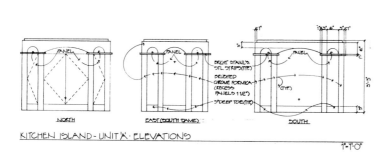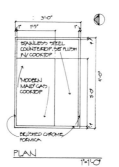

PANEL

NORTH

PANEL

EAST (SOUTH SAME)

BRIGHT STAINL'S
STL. STRIP (TYP)

BRUSHED
CHROME FORMICA
(RECESS
PANELS 1 1/2")

3" DEEP TOE (TYP)

PANEL

SOUTH

STAINLESS STEEL
COUNTERTOP, SET FLUSH
W/ COOKTOP

'MODERN
MAID' GAS
COOKTOP

BRUSHED CHROME
FORMICA

PLAN

KITCHEN ISLAND - UNIT 'A' - ELEVATIONS   1"=1'-0"

PLAN   1"=1'-0"

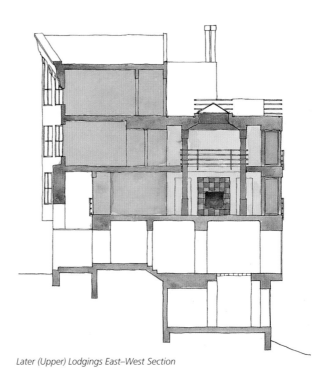

Later (Upper) Lodgings East–West Section

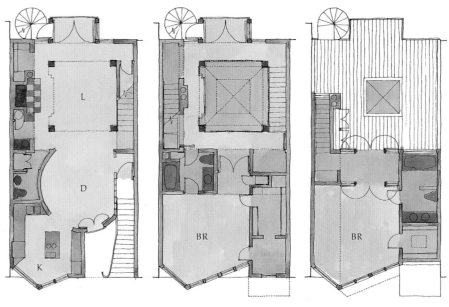

Third Level   *Fourth Level*   *Fifth Level*

Querio Residence
Oakland, California

The late architectural historian David Gebhard observed of his hometown, Santa Barbara, that its ubiquitous Spanish Colonial Revival character is, in fact, established by just a fraction of its buildings. The County Courthouse, Fox Arlington Theatre, Paseo, etc., are exuberantly styled; many others are plain, though sharing in the architectural vocabulary of the place, including pale stucco walls, red clay tile roofs, etc.

If the Oakland Hills are not Santa Barbara (though they are styled a good deal more "Spanish" today than before the 1991 firestorm), the idea that a single building might knit together the understated stylistic threads of its neighbors, and so relate a group of previously disparate buildings, has its appeal.

This house's steep, upsloping site is in the midst of a modest neighborhood, builder-built from the 1920s through the 1960s. While later houses are mildly modern, earlier examples include white stucco walls, spots of lush planting, and red concrete walks, and they are vaguely "Spanish." This house amplifies these *sotto voce* parts, as well as employing the *basso profundo* stylistic devices of the Spanish Colonial Revival, including a Churrigueresque-esque balcony, great scalloped window, and Moorish chimney tower. Inside, the more public spaces are arranged in a single, long room, alongside a small court, facing the Bay. Private rooms are held away from the street, at the back of the court.

The house burned to its foundations in the 1991 firestorm. Its inhabitants, surviving unharmed, chose not to rebuild, and today a much different house rests on the same foundations, indifferent to its neighbors.

The late Charles Moore, when told that the magical interiors of his tiny former house in New Haven, Connecticut had been remodeled out of existence, was pleased and without regret. He said, "It's even better this way" by which he may have meant that the memory of the place is even more vivid and compelling than the place itself had ever been.

1. *Living Room*
2. *Dining Room*
3. *Kitchen*
4. *Bedroom*
5. *Family Room*
6. *Courtyard*
7. *Master Bedroom*

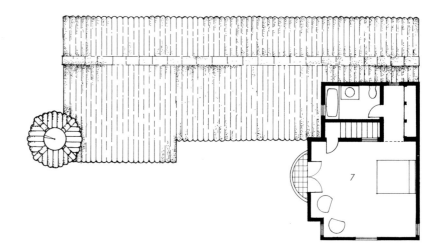

Upper Floor

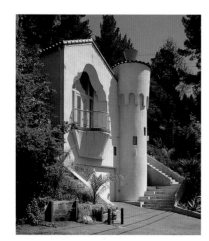

Main Floor

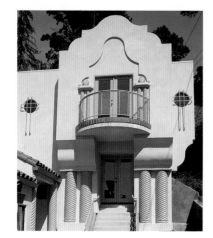

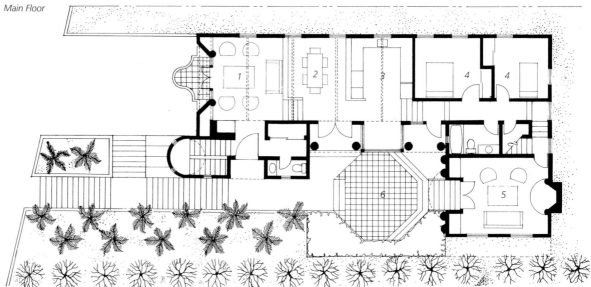

Left: *Just the shell of the tower remains following 1991 Oakland Hills Firestorm.*

Opposite Page Above: *Turreted corner tower/chimney houses circular stairs.*
Below: *West-facing courtyard wall is fashioned neo-Churriguresque.*

Right: Wide stairs lead from Broadway terrace to the courtyard beyond.

Opposite Page Above: View from balcony overlooking the courtyard, along the terra cotta hued clay tile roof, towards San Francisco Bay.
Below: Entrance is flanked by a pair or round windows with painted steel grilles.

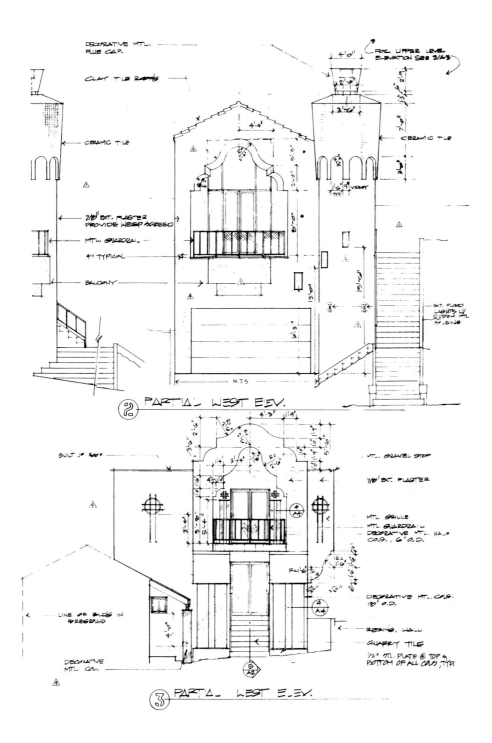

DECORATIVE MTL. FLUE CAP.

CLAY TILE ROOFS

CERAMIC TILE

7/8" EXT. PLASTER PROVIDE WEEP SCREED

MTL. GUARDRAIL

4" TYPICAL

BALCONY

FOR UPPER LEVEL ELEVATION SEE 3/A3

CERAMIC TILE

EXT. FLOOD LIGHTS W/ CUSTOM MTL. HOUSING

N.T.S

2 PARTIAL WEST ELEV.

BUILT UP ROOF

LINE OF BLDG IN FOREGROUND

DECORATIVE MTL. COL.

MTL. GRAVEL STOP

7/8" EXT. PLASTER

MTL. GRILLE
MTL. GUARDRAIL
DECORATIVE MTL. HALF COLS., 6" O.D.

DECORATIVE MTL. COLS. 18" O.D.

RETNG. WALL

QUARRY TILE

1/2" MTL. PLATE @ TOP & BOTTOM OF ALL COLS. TYP.

3 PARTIAL WEST ELEV.

Right Above: _The floor of the room contain-ing, living, dining, and kitchen rises with the slope of the site._ **_Middle:_** _Kitchen._ **_Below:_** _Ceiling is supported on wooden trusses, whose pieces are fitted together with iron straps._

Opposite Page: _The line of doors and glazing is held behind a highly figured exterior opening-a favored device of early Bay Region Style architects._

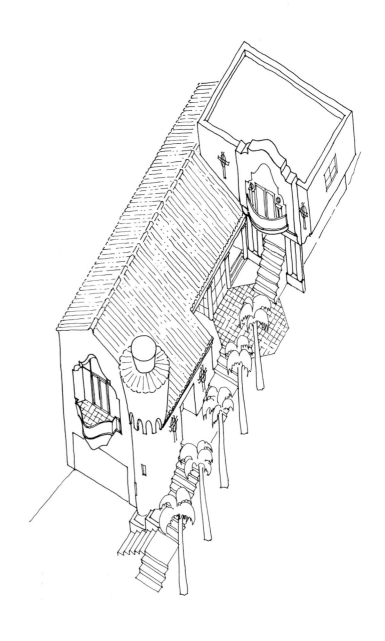

Right: Terra cotta-tiled hall and stairs lead to entrance beyond.

Opposite Page Above: Fireplace at study is a miniature of the house's courtyard-facing façade. **Below:** Stairs and floor levels adhere to the contours of the site.

7007 Bluy Terrace

Rancho Diablo

Lafayette, California

Many of the planet's most compelling places enthrall us not only with their sunlit, masterly, and correct architectural forms; the drama of their sites; and grand, vivid, as well as intimate spaces; but also with their histories. Simple, unassuming buildings, when possessed of pasts sufficiently evocative, offer experiences as rich as places more magnificent; and, even at this late point, the ruined Forum in Rome exercises our imaginations more thoroughly and remains more rewarding than the fully-intact Forum Shops at Caesar's Palace in Las Vegas.

An irony attending preservation of old buildings is that the more renewed they appear, the less accessible are their histories to our imaginations. The textures and possibilities of the past may be lost to too much renovation and fresh paint. The elaborate, polychromatic drawings reconstructing the Roman Forum in its heyday are never so moving as its still remains.

Rancho Diablo, when we came to it, was a house with a past; and it was a ruin, though at a domestic rather than imperial scale. The house had belonged to a great women's tennis champion of the 1920s, though she had never lived there and did not care for the place. It had been built by her father, a doctor, in 1930, employing the services of Berkeley architect Lillian Bridgman, for his mistress and himself, on a large and then remote tract of land.

With the house were a variety of stories—of the mistress sitting on the verandah cradling a squirrel gun; of the missing tax collector; of the hidden cache of gold coins; and, of course, the ghost. Two of the house's most recent, and wholly sober, inhabitants had looked upon the shade of the mistress, seated, up on the verandah.

Our idea, in restoring the house, inventing a landscape where none had been contrived, and fully reconstructing an out-building, was to make the place more like itself than it had ever been. With the house, careless additions were removed; surfaces cleaned and repaired, but never refinished; and new systems (HVAC, electrical, etc.) invisibly installed. A garden of "Old" California inspiration was installed, including palms, cacti, and shrubs with names like "coyote bush." The outbuilding, to which the mistress repaired when the doctor invited friends (to preserve the fiction, in a time when appearances mattered, that she was the housekeeper), was remade in vertical, whitewashed redwood boards and reworked to house the owners' extensive collection of souvenir building miniatures.

Those visiting the place for the first time wonder what was done; those who last saw the house dilapidated barely recognize it. Unexplained flashes of light, reported by the house's new inhabitants for the first year, have, with time, diminished.

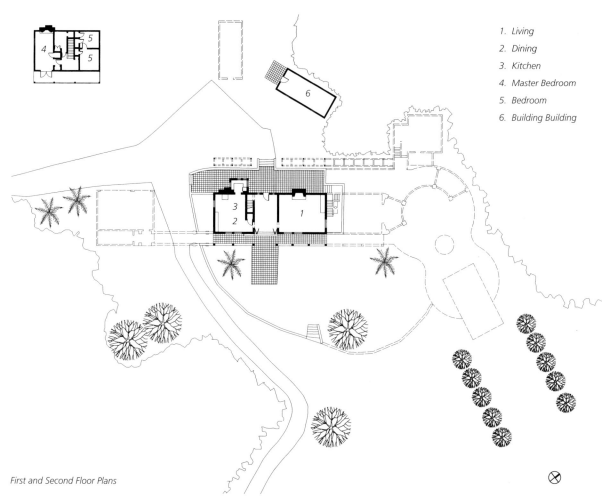

1. Living
2. Dining
3. Kitchen
4. Master Bedroom
5. Bedroom
6. Building Building

First and Second Floor Plans

This Page: The landscape adjacent to the house, never developed before, is now worked up as a palm and cactus garden.

Opposite Page Above: Interior and exterior door and window frames had been made up from 12-inch (30-centimeter) square redwood timbers. **Below:** At entrance, redwood timber framed door, arched brick window with forged metal grille, and redwood board-and-batten siding at second story.

Right: *Living room ceiling is made from redwood beams and decking; walls are white-stained brick; and floor is quarry tile.*

Opposite Page Above: *Living room is furnished with forged iron light fixtures; "eye dazzler" Navaho rugs; patterned ceramic tile tables; and cowhide and flamestitch fabric chairs and couch.* **Below:** *Dining room curtains are from three colors of leather. Furniture is ca. 1930 "Monterey," produced in California.*

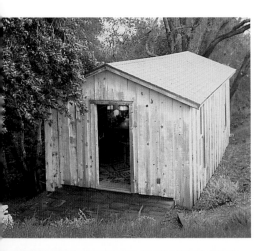

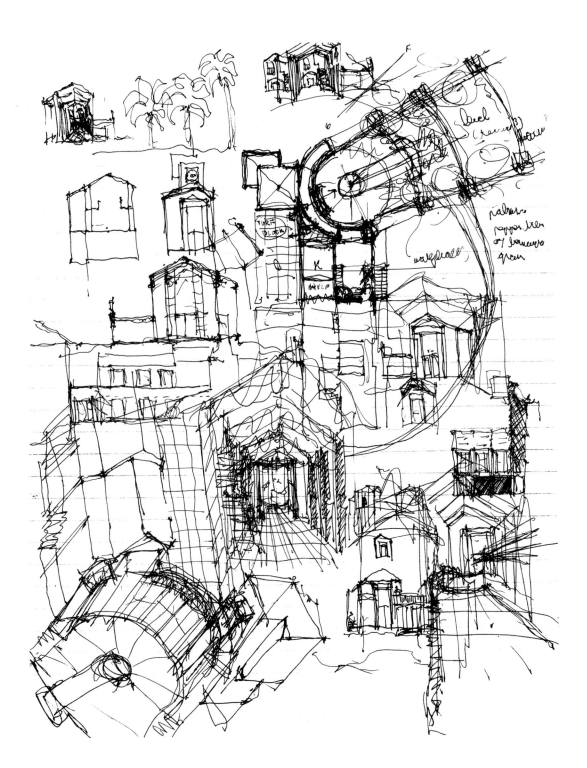

Left: *Interior of "building building" is fitted with resawn fir plywood ceiling and walls and vertical grain fir floor and shelves. It houses the world's most extensive collection of souvenir building miniatures.*

Opposite Page: *Whitewashed vertical board on board exterior of "building building."*

Right: *Among souvenir building miniatures in the collection are these (left to right): Colonne d'Austerlitz, Paris; Water Cascade, Kassel; Luxor Obelisk, Paris; unidentified Egyptian obelisk; Erechtheum, Athens; Theseum, Athens; and the Temple of Hercules, Rome.*

Opposite Page: *"Building building."*

Tabancay/Austin Residence

Berkeley, California

Beginning in the 1820s in England, there was what now seems a narrow debate over the proper style for church architecture. The Ecclesiologists, including A.W.N. Pugin, argued for the Middle Pointed Gothic of the eleventh and twelfth centuries, citing it as straightforward, yet not crude; traditional, but continuous with a Catholic past. Others spoke for the Perpendicular Gothic of the fourteenth century, championing its refinements, which Pugin, *et al*, thought inappropriately ornate.

If history largely condescends in its treatment of these and other skirmishes in the Style Wars, and if the force of these arguments now seems remote, the truth is that debates over style are almost always debates over substance.

Jefferson's passion for Roman architectural forms, via Palladio, includes belief in their appropriateness for a new republic. To those who doubt the capacity of architectural styles to carry cultural meanings, we suggest imagining the University of Virginia gotten up in Perpendicular Gothic.

Early in this century, some modernists were excited with the possibilities suggested by buildings thought altogether free of style—grain elevators, bridges and dams, industrial plants, etc. Here, they thought, were strictly purposeful architectural forms, not frivolous or arbitrary, unencumbered by the manners of the past. That the pursuit of an astylar modernism quickly congealed into the doctrinaire banalities of the International style is a tale often told.

Underreported is the truth that style is an inevitable, intrinsic part of architecture; that almost all buildings appear styled, even grain elevators; and that architectural style is freighted with meanings. With houses, of course, these meanings may be more personal than widely cultural.

For this addition and remodeling to their nearly astylar, 1940s, wood-sided, builder-designed house in the Berkeley Hills, our clients imagined domes and minarets; Moorish arches and patterned tile work; gauzy curtains and flickering, pierced brass lanterns—all having to do with their memories of movie theaters with names like Alhambra; with the filmic travels of Sinbad the sailor; and with *1001 Arabian Nights*. That they saw so much in so little remains, for us, the project's chief astonishment.

A new entry tower, facing the street, is topped by a copper-finished dome, supported on wooden beams carved to resemble Moorish dragons, At night, from outside, the tower glows, becoming a lantern. Inside, furniture is from polychromatically-finished plywood and etched and carved glass. The saturated hues of diaphanous curtains are repeated in pillows set about the floor in an octagonal tower facing the back garden and Bay. Overhead, a gleaming brass lamp is suspended beneath a vivid blue-painted dome.

When Santayana observed that "Those who cannot remember the past are condemned to repeat it," he must not have been thinking of architects. The rich history of architectural appearances, of styles and all they evoke, is a bright flame about which we are bound to flutter.

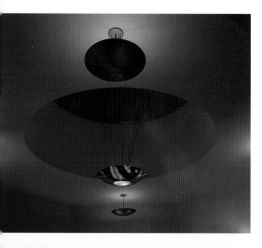

Pleasure dome

Left: Entry tower with adjacent minaret-shaped chimney are finished in integrally colored stucco. Arch-shaped door surround is made of ceramic tile.

Opposite Page Above: Ceiling of "pleasure dome" detail. *Below:* Beyond living/dining area, through a screen of pointed arches, is the "pleasure dome."

Following Spread: View of the house from Hillcrest Drive.

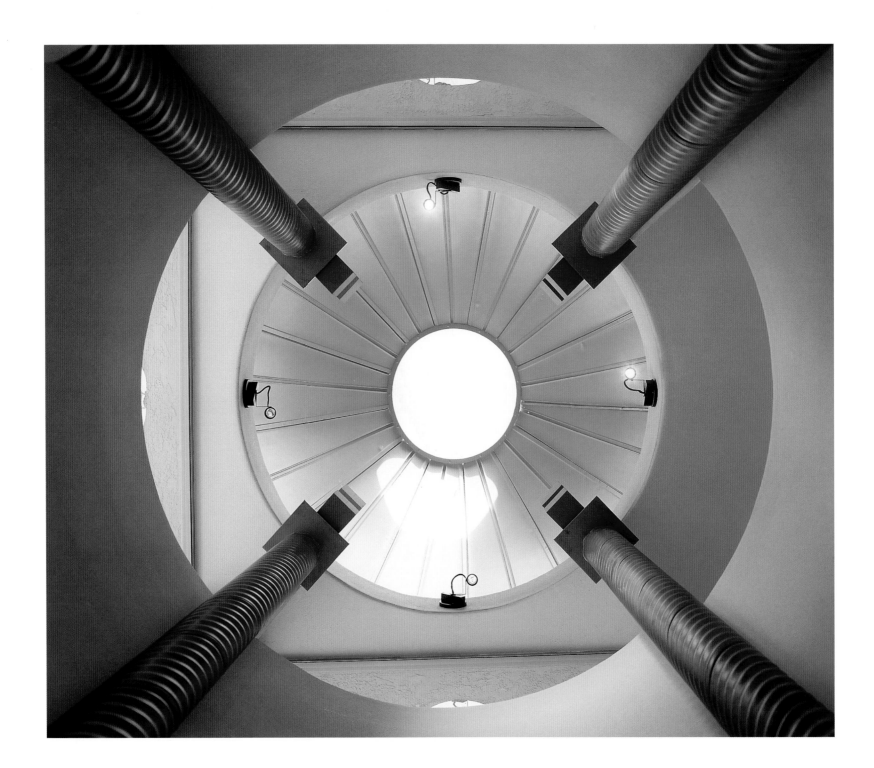

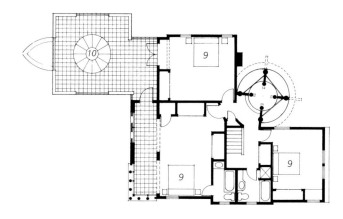

Upper Level Plan

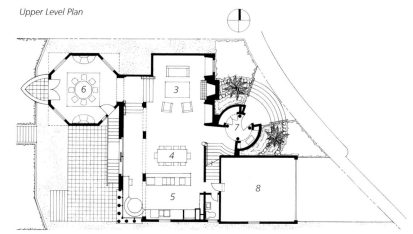

Middle Level Plan

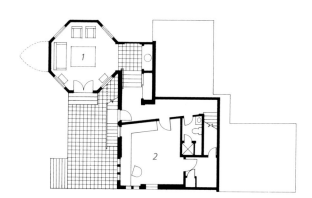

Lower Level Plan

1. Family Room
2. Study
3. Living
4. Dining
5. Kitchen
6. Pleasure Dome
7. Entry
8. Garage
9. Bedroom
10. Roof Deck

Left Above: Dome at entry tower is copper-finished, prefabricated agricultural silo roof.
Middle: Wood beam ends at entry suggest dragons. **Below:** Ceramic mosaic floor at entry includes spiral of gold tiles.

Opposite Page: Interior of entry tower dome.

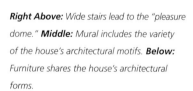

Right Above: *Wide stairs lead to the "pleasure dome."* **Middle:** *Mural includes the variety of the house's architectural motifs.* **Below:** *Furniture shares the house's architectural forms.*

Opposite Page: *View from the "pleasure dome," up wide stairs, to the living room fireplace, with patterned ceramic tile surround.*

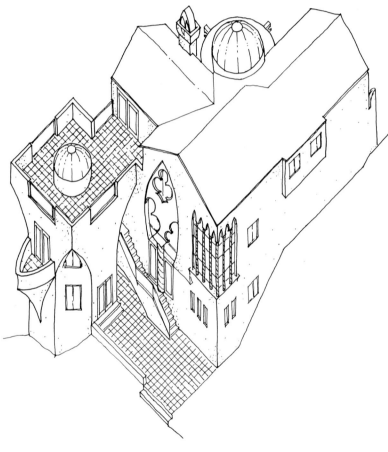

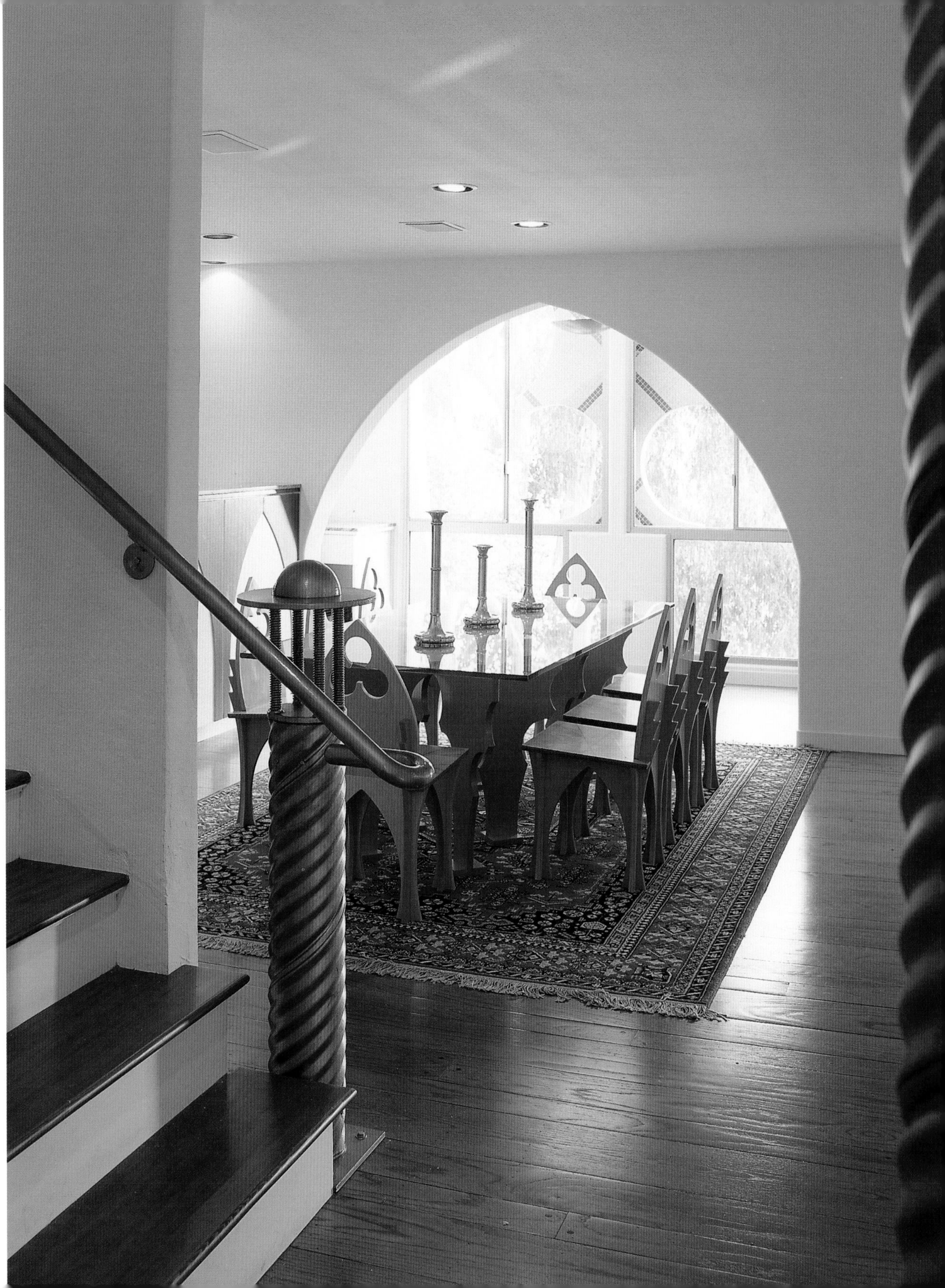

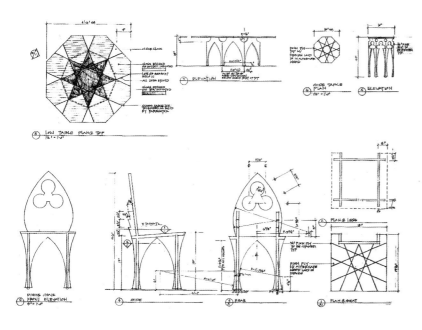

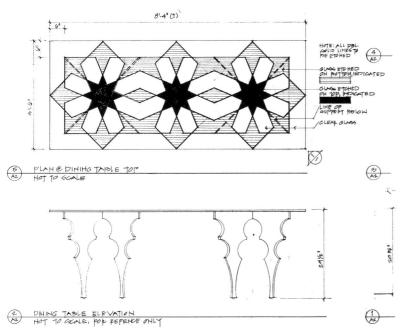

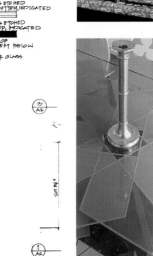

Left Above: *View through ceramic tile trefoil.*
Middle: *Color-stained plywood chair incorporates the house's architectural motifs.* **Below:** *Arabic-patterned, carved and etched glass table.*

Opposite Page: *Pointed arch frames view toward Bay beyond.*

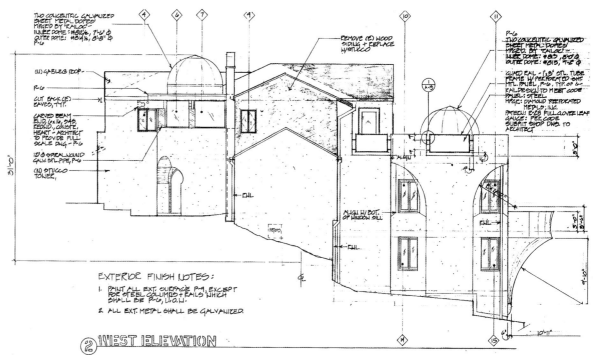

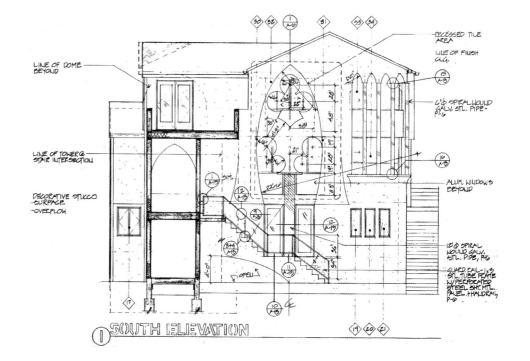

EXTERIOR FINISH NOTES:

1. PAINT ALL EXT. SURFACE P-9, EXCEPT FOR STEEL COLUMNS + RAILS WHICH SHALL BE P-6, U.O.N.

2. ALL EXT. METAL SHALL BE GALVANIZED.

WEST ELEVATION

SOUTH ELEVATION

TWO CONCENTRIC GALVANIZED SHEET METAL DOMES MFG'D BY "RAILOC" INNER DOME: #812½, 7'-6" ∅ OUTER DOME: #814½, 8'-3" ∅ P-6

(N) GABLED ROOF

P-6

CUT BACK (E) EAVES, TYP.

CARVED BEAM END, 6x16, 248, REDWD, CONST, HEART - ARCHITECT TO PROVIDE FULL SCALE DWG - P-6

12" ∅ SPIRAL WOUND GALV. STL. PIPE, P-6

(N) STUCCO TOWER

REMOVE (E) WOOD SIDING + REPLACE W/STUCCO

ALIGN W/ BOT. OF WINDOW SILL

P-6 TWO CONCENTRIC GALVANIZED SHEET METAL DOMES MFG'D. BY "RAILOC" INNER DOME: #813, 8'-0" ∅ OUTER DOME: #813, 7'-6" ∅

GUARD RAIL - 1½" ∅ STL. TUBE FRAME W/PERFORATED SHT. MTL. PANEL, P-6, TYP. OF 6 - RAIL DESIGN TO MEET CODE PANEL: STEEL MFG'C: DIAMOND PERFORATED METALS, INC. PATTERN: R-28 FULL CLOVER LEAF GAUGE: PER CODE SUBMIT SHOP DWG. TO ARCHITECT

RECESSED TILE AREA

LINE OF FINISH CLG.

6" ∅ SPIRAL WOUND GALV. STL. PIPE - P-6

ALUM. WINDOWS BEYOND

12" ∅ SPIRAL WOUND GALV. STL. PIPE, P-6

GUARD RAIL - 1½" ∅ STL. TUBE FRAME W/PERFORATED STEEL SHT. MTL. PANEL + HANDRAIL, P-6

LINE OF DOME BEYOND

LINE OF TOWER @ STAIR INTERSECTION

DECORATIVE STUCCO SURFACE

OVERFLOW

Left: *Attenuated, spirally-wound metal columns stretch two stories.*

Opposite Page Above: *Columns are finished in copper-pigmented paint.*
Below: *Breakfast alcove.*

Jordan Residence

Oakland, California

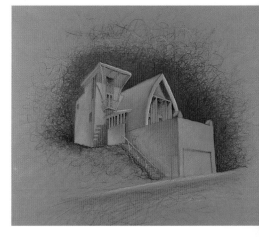

Opposite Page: *This small house rises along with its steep site. The first level and tower are tunnel dash finished stucco; the main floor features acid-etched, copper-faced asphalt shingles. The tower roof and entry trellis are painted and unfinished wood.*

With the design of houses, what is the place of fun? In the serious work of architecture, where is there room for the frivolous? Of course, entertainment, which some relate to fun, is big business, transacted in entertaining-enough-looking places, from City Walk in Los Angeles, to Downtown Disney in Orlando, to almost all of the "new" Las Vegas and Times Square. Marxists might mutter about the commodification of fun. In fact, much of the fun in architecture now is associated with "venues," apparently at the expense of more everyday places. Where, for example, is the fun in all the neo-traditional new towns? Where is the celebration at Celebration?

Making fun is often a sober enterprise. Ironically, comedians and the makers of funny films, books, and buildings wring their hands over being taken seriously—while their melancholy peers make off with all the prizes.

When we presented the first scheme for this little house, which we'd imagined as an economical arrangement of boxy pieces at various scales, our client responded that it was "not fun enough." It looked, she added, like "an elegant trailer."

Regrouped back at the drawing board, we settled on another approach, a conceit, relying on an imagined coincidence between this project and Bernard Maybeck's lost Hearst Hall, completed in 1899, which housed a University of California women's organization. Our client publishes a newspaper; Phoebe Hearst was connected to the publishing game. Our client's former house had burned in the 1991 Oakland Hills firestorm; Hearst Hall was consumed by fire in 1922.

The new scheme (found fully fun enough), like Hearst Hall, includes a central, "Gothicky" vaulted volume, supported on wooden ribs. At Hearst Hall, a pair of towers flanked this room. We managed a single tower, containing the daughter's bedroom, on the narrow site.

Several steps up from the arch-vaulted living room, the dining room and kitchen open to a quiet patio, through an over-scaled redwood trellis whose pieces are carved to resemble dragons' heads. Beyond, a charred live oak is, again, green.

One weekend, during construction, when the framing was just complete, a critic installed on the project a large, carefully lettered sign, facing the street—"Chapel with Outhouse 1993"—a clever comment on the apparent form of the house, as well as the place's artistic ambitions. Others, choosing more conventional forums such as letters to the editor, described the house as the "lizard-skinned taqueria" and, best of both worlds, "lizard-skinned chapel with taqueria." With houses, apparently, fun is not for everyone.

Yet, the evening of her first Halloween in the new house, our client noted that an unusual number of her grown-up neighbors appeared on her porch, not for a trick or a treat, but for a glimpse inside her fun house.

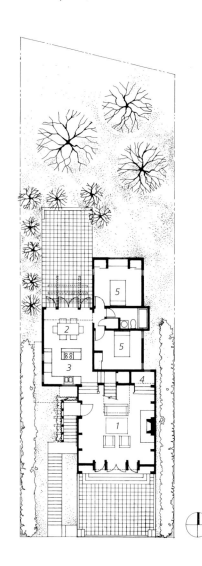

1. *Living Room*
2. *Dining*
3. *Kitchen*
4. *Study Alcove*
5. *Bedroom*
6. *Open to Below*

Main Floor

Upper Floor

Left: Construction photographs.

Opposite Page: Archival photographs of the exterior and interior of Bernard Maybeck's 1899 Hearst Hall.

Right: Jordan Residence was among the earliest houses to rise in the wake of the 1991 Oakland Hills Firestorm. Note adjacent stairs leading to bare foundations, and seared trees.

Opposite Page Above: *Animal-shaped redwood beams support the entry roof.*
Below: *Trellis at garden entrance.*

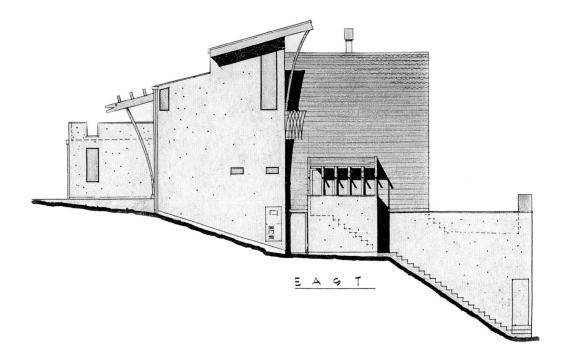

E A S T

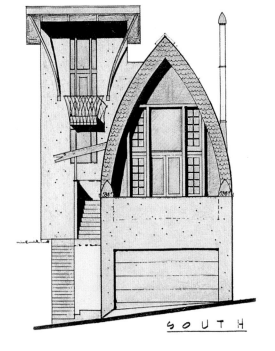

S O U T H

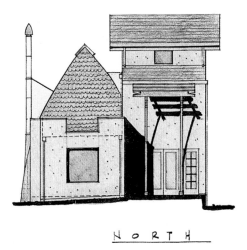

N O R T H

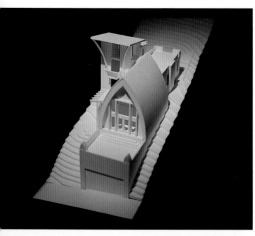

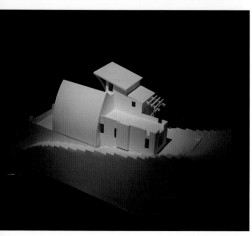

Left: *Overscaled entrance to living from terrace.*

Opposite Page: *Study model, of cream-colored museum board with a grey Strathmore board base shows the site's topography, and the house's two scales—larger toward the street, more intimate toward the back patio.*

Right: *View toward the living room from the top landing of winding, overhanging stairs, with "minstrel's balcony" in the foreground, and an integrally colored concrete terrace beyond. Suspended light fixtures whose forms are miniatures of the volume of the room, are of copper screen.*

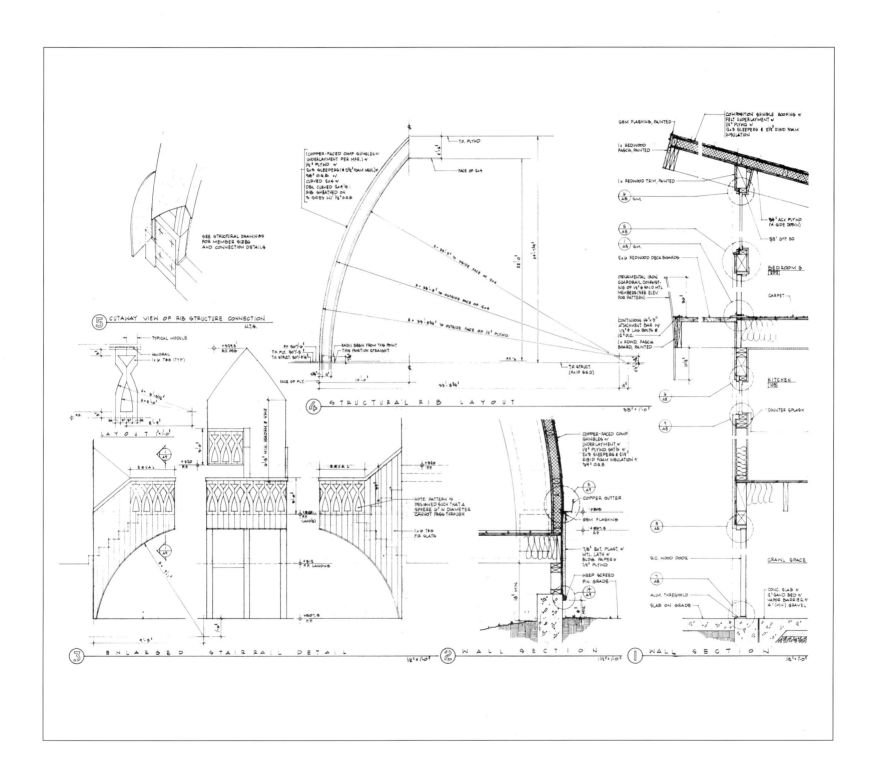

SEE STRUCTURAL DRAWINGS
FOR MEMBER SIZES
AND CONNECTION DETAILS

COMPOSITION SHINGLE ROOFING W/
FELT UNDERLAYMENT W/
1/2" PLYWD W/
2x3 SLEEPERS @ 2 1/2" RIGID FOAM
INSULATION

GSM FLASHING, PAINTED

1x REDWOOD
FASCIA, PAINTED

1x REDWOOD TRIM, PAINTED

6/A8 SIM.

5/A8
1/A8 SIM.

3/4" ACX PLYWD
(A SIDE DOWN)

3/8" GYP. BD.

2x6 REDWOOD DECK BOARDS

BEDROOM 3

ORNAMENTAL IRON
GUARDRAIL CONSIST-
ING OF 1/2"Ø SOLID MTL.
MEMBERS (SEE ELEV.
FOR PATTERN)

CARPET

CONTINUOUS 1/4"x3"
ATTACHMENT BAR W/
1/2"Ø LAG BOLTS @
18" O.C.
1x RDWD. FASCIA
BOARD, PAINTED

6/A8

KITCHEN

9/A8

COUNTER SPLASH

⑤ CUTAWAY VIEW OF RIB STRUCTURE CONNECTION
N.T.S.

TYPICAL MODULE

HANDRAIL
1x6 T&G (TYP.)

LAYOUT 1"=1'-0"

(COPPER-FACED COMP SHINGLES W/
UNDERLAYMENT PER MFR.) W/
1/2" PLYWD W/
2x6 SLEEPERS (@ 2 1/2" FOAM NAIL) W/
3/4" O.S.B. W/
CURVED 2x4 W/
DBL CURVED 2x4'S:
RIB SHEATHED ON
3 SIDES W/ 1/2" O.S.B.

RADII BEGIN FROM THIS POINT
THIS PORTION STRAIGHT

FF BOT-9
T.O. PLY. BOT-8
T.O. STRUCT. BOT-4 1/4"

FACE OF PLY.

10'-0"

T.O. PLYND

FACE OF 2x4

R=39'-9" TO INSIDE FACE OF 2x4

R=39'-8" TO OUTSIDE FACE OF 2x4

R=39'-8 3/8" TO OUTSIDE FACE OF 1/2" PLYND.

RB

T.O. STRUCT.
(4x10 B.G.D)

33'-8 3/4"

④ STRUCTURAL RIB LAYOUT
3/8" = 1'-0"

EQUAL

+990
RB

+990
RB

EQUAL

+B10
RB
(LANDG)

6'-8" MIN. HEADRM @ STAIR

NOTE: PATTERN IS
DESIGNED SUCH THAT A
SPHERE 6" IN DIAMETER
CANNOT PASS THROUGH

1x6 T&G
FIR SLATS

A8

A8

+813
RB
F.F. LANDING

+807.5
RB

9'-6"

COPPER-FACED COMP.
SHINGLES W/
UNDERLAYMENT W/
1/2" PLYWD. SHT'G W/
2x3 SLEEPERS @ 2 1/2"
RIGID FOAM INSULATION W/
3/4" O.S.B.

5/A9

COPPER GUTTER

+813

GSM FLASHING

7/8" EXT. PLAST. W/
MTL. LATH W/
BLDG. PAPER W/
1/2" PLYND

WEEP SCREED
FIN. GRADE

14/A9

16" MIN.

G.C. WOOD DOOR

7/A9

ALUM. THRESHOLD

SLAB ON GRADE

CRAWL SPACE

5/A8

CONC. SLAB W/
2" SAND BED W/
VAPOR BARRIER W/
4" (MIN) GRAVEL

③ ENLARGED STAIR RAIL DETAIL
1/2" = 1'-0"

② WALL SECTION
1 1/2" = 1'-0"

① WALL SECTION
1 1/2" = 1'-0"

Right: *The "Gothicky" living room is supported on beams made up from oriented strand board fixed to a simple wood frame (glue laminated beams proved too expensive). The ceiling and walls, also made from oriented strand board, are color stained.*

Opposite Page: *The fireplace surround employs the copper-faced asphalt shingles of the exterior, as well as copper-finished ceramic tile. The lighter, patterned ceramic tile is from the owner's previous house, which burned to its foundations.*

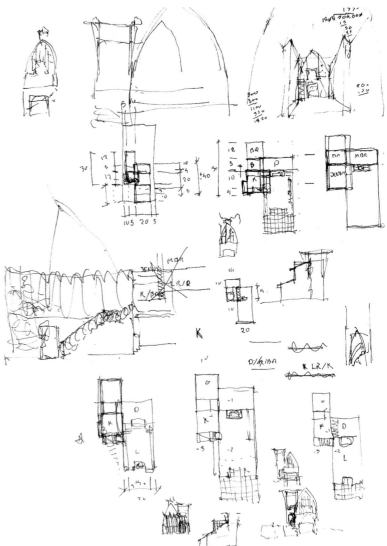

Allen Residence
Oakland, California

Above: Entry tower is framed in parallam wood posts, cantilevered up to support free-form roof canopy.

Opposite Page: The curve of the house follows the arc of an automobile's path, along the roof, to the garage.

New buildings are almost always styled on older buildings. Athens' Parthenon, with progeny from Rome to Nashville, spanning twenty-five centuries, emulates still more ancient constructions built up out of rough logs and timbers. Architectural history may be thought a species of genealogy, tracing roots, recording marriages fruitful or not, and observing the paths of offspring.

An underappreciated branch of this family includes buildings whose origins are not wholly architectural, but which look to other sources. Among these impure structures are those the late architectural historian David Gebhard identified as "programmatic"—hot dog stands shaped like hot dogs, for instance.

There are subtler examples. At least since the fifth century, many Christian churches have been arranged around a symbolically charged cruciform plan; by the eighteenth century, certain Baroque church interiors appeared modeled on Heaven itself, complete with swirling clouds, angels, and recreated materials. In our own time, the Eero Saarinen-designed TWA Terminal in New York is styled, appropriately enough, on avian forms.

An intent in reaching outside the traditional architectural vocabulary, whether for an airport terminal, church, or hot dog stand, is to make places more familiar and accessible to our interests. Against the backdrop of many places whose meanings, if any, are fully encrypted, programmatic architecture appears an almost practical approach.

Houses, more than any other type of building, are often thought of and described in ways approximately programmatic, rather than traditionally architectural. Kent Bloomer, for example, has described this imagery based on the human body, including the hearth as heart, attic as head containing memory, and façade as face.

Some German Expressionist-inspired films, as well as Walt Disney's earlier pictures, feature houses almost fiercely physiognomic, whose furnishings appear nearly alive.

The design of this house, set in a part of the Oakland Hills remote from any architectural context, is abstracted and collaged from the features of its site, rather than from other buildings. The twisting drive reflects the nearby street; the vivid blue curvilinear canopy and adjacent green-stained poles are related to the surrounding eucalyptus forest and sky and clouds overhead; the garage shed restates a predominant form of houses nearby, but unseen. The colors of the place are both complementary and nearly identical to the colors of the site.

Entrance to the house is via bridge to a glazed tower. Inside, a single space under a climbing, fan-shaped ceiling, supports the place's more public purposes and is a platform for distant forest views. Private rooms are reached down stairs. Unsurprisingly, with its curvilinear, open-planned, brightly-colored forms, this house is often thought Modern. Its roots, though, run to a hot dog stand in West L.A.

1. Driveway
2. Garage
3. Entry
4. Living Area
5. Dining Area
6. Kitchen
7. Master Bedroom
8. Den
9. Bedroom

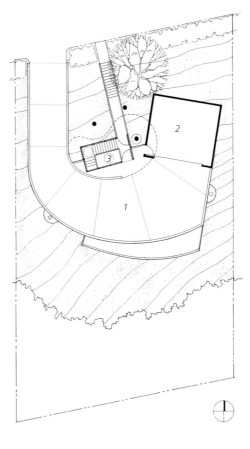

Entry Level Plan

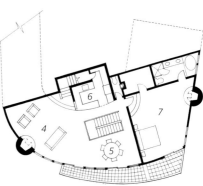

Middle Level Plan

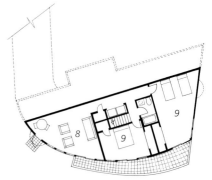

Lower Level Plan

Left: *A pipe-rail-edged bridge leads from Skyline Drive, between flanking poles, under a swirling blue canopy, to the entry tower.*

Opposite Page: *The garage is sheathed in patinated copper-faced roll roofing.*

Right: *Overhead view of entry tower interior.*

Opposite Page: *Entry tower windows are set within the painted wood structural grid.*

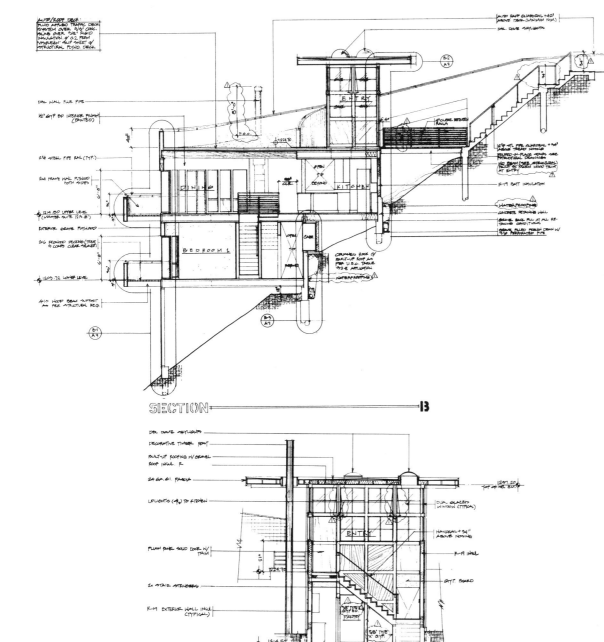

SECTION ━━━━━━━━━━━━━━━━━━━━ B

SECTION ━━━━━━━━━━━━━━━━━ C

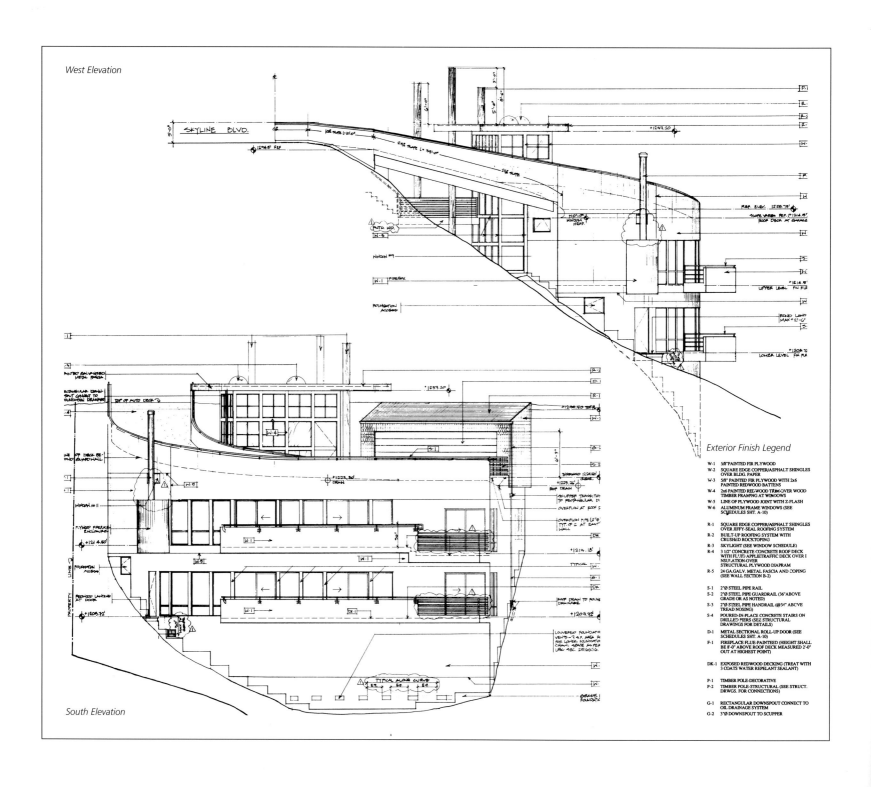

West Elevation

SKYLINE BLVD.

South Elevation

Exterior Finish Legend

W-1 5/8" PAINTED FIR PLYWOOD

W-2 SQUARE EDGE COPPER/ASPHALT SHINGLES OVER BLDG. PAPER

W-3 5/8" PAINTED FIR PLYWOOD WITH 2x6 PAINTED REDWOOD BATTENS

W-4 2x6 PAINTED REDWOOD TRIM OVER WOOD TIMBER FRAMING AT WINDOWS

W-5 LINE OF PLYWOOD JOINT WITH Z-FLASH

W-6 ALUMINUM FRAME WINDOWS (SEE SCHEDULES SHT. A-10)

R-1 SQUARE EDGE COPPER/ASPHALT SHINGLES OVER JIFFY-SEAL ROOFING SYSTEM

R-2 BUILT-UP ROOFING SYSTEM WITH CRUSHED ROCKTOPING

R-3 SKYLIGHT (SEE WINDOW SCHEDULE)

R-4 3 1/2" CONCRETE ROOF DECK WITH FL/JD APPLIETRAFFIC DECK OVER 1 INSULATION OVER STRUCTURAL PLYWOOD DIAPRAM

R-5 24 GA.GALV. METAL FASCIA AND COPING (SEE WALL SECTION B-2)

S-1 2"Ø STEEL PIPE RAIL

S-2 2"Ø STEEL PIPE GUARDRAIL (36"ABOVE GRADE OR AS NOTED)

S-3 2"Ø STEEL PIPE HANDRAIL (@34" ABOVE TREAD NOSING)

S-4 POURED-IN-PLACE CONCRETE STAIRS ON DRILLED PIERS (SEE STRUCTURAL DRAWINGS FOR DETAILS)

D-1 METAL SECTIONAL ROLL-UP DOOR (SEE SCHEDULES SHT. A-10)

F-1 FIREPLACE FLUE-PAINTEED (HEIGHT SHALL BE 8'-0" ABOVE ROOF DECK MEASURED 2'-0" OUT AT HIGHEST POINT)

DK-1 EXPOSED REDWOOD DECKING (TREAT WITH 3 COATS WATER REPELANT SEALANT)

P-1 TIMBER POLE-DECORATIVE

P-2 TIMBER POLE-STRUCTURAL (SEE STRUCT. DRWGS. FOR CONNECTIONS)

G-1 RECTANGULAR DOWNSPOUT CONNECT TO OIL DRAINAGE SYSTEM

G-2 3"Ø DOWNSPOUT TO SCUPPER

Left: *House's curved form is reiterated in arc-shaped balconies and fireplace drum. Hue of integrally colored stucco walls is complementary to the green of the surrounding eucalyptus forest.*

Right: Decks, on two levels, face the adjacent eucalyptus forest.

Opposite Page Above: Model. *Below:* Colored glass panel at entrance door portrays the house's plan.

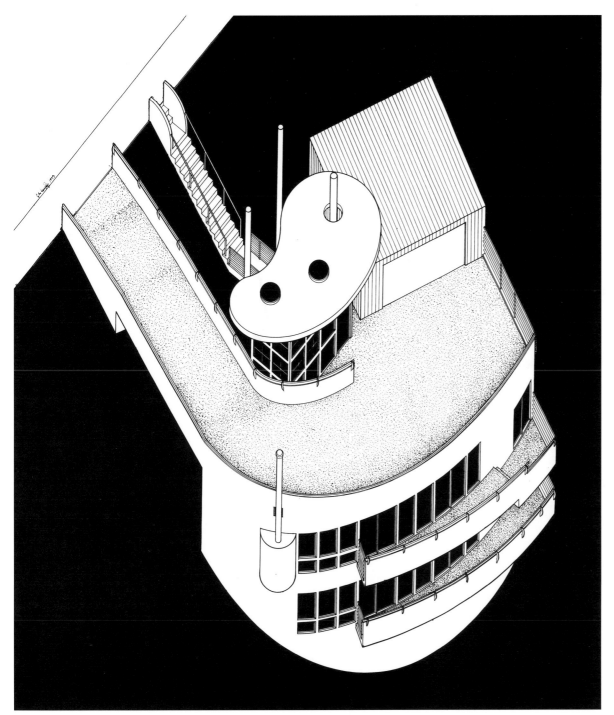

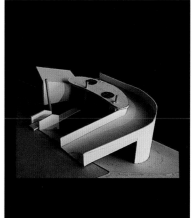

Right: *Living and dining are within a single large room, beneath a spiraling ceiling, fashioned from glue-laminated beams and oriented strand board.*

Opposite Page: *Slope of the ceiling follows the pitch of the driveway above. Beyond pipe railed stair enclosure is a compact kitchen, set at the base of the entry tower.*

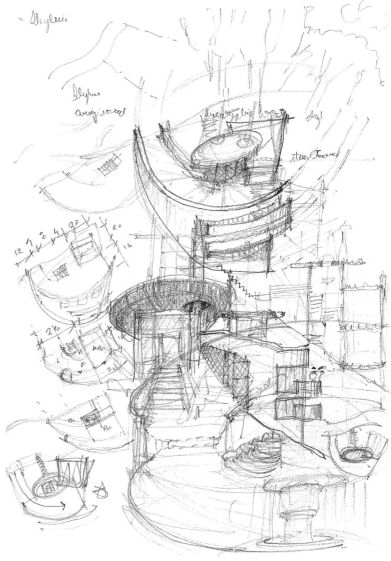

House on Twin Peaks

San Francisco, California

I f the dry journals of architectural history and lush, glossy shelter magazines share an ardor for places realized in a single style—Gothic or Googie; Moorish, Modern, or Minimal; Louis this or that; etc.—the places many of us inhabit, especially when touched by our own eccentricities, are both less pure and more singular.

Houses are often said to reflect tastes, as well as interests, temperaments, even personalities. However, with the most appealing houses, inhabited by the most vivid personalities—Soane's London townhouse, Jefferson's Monticello, Will Rogers' Pacific Palisades ranch, even Elvis' Graceland—this reflection seems less the point, and more an intriguing side effect. With the design of these places, one imagines Soane's passion for the *lumiere mysterieuse* and Elvis' for avocado-hued shag carpeting as originating in belief, rather than in desires to provide clues for contemporary and later Sherlocks.

Among the most famous and extensive houses hewing to their inhabitant's ambitious and changing sets of interests is Hadrian's Villa. That it is much ruined has only, for many, expanded the wondrous possibilities of the place. Still, it seems certain that Hadrian's travels to the ends of an empire including Egypt, Syria, Constantinople, Greece, North Africa, and Spain sparked much of the expanding, combining variety of this place's forms.

If the scale of the Emperor's undertakings is now unavailable, except to Internet plutocrats, tycoons and other despots, the opportunity remains to make congenial and responsive places, suitably complex and impure.

This house is arranged with two others on a large, rustic site, overlooking San Francisco and the Bay; it was our client's boyhood home. An existing cabin had been built by his parents in the 1940s, and they had moved a small cottage and dairy barn to the site in the 1950s. His sister lives in the cabin, and a grown son in the cottage.

The renovation and addition to the barn coincided with our client's returning from a financial career in New York. In the world outside of San Francisco, he had grown fond of Mexico, where business was often conducted, and of Japan. Over time, an enthusiasm and eye for Modern art and furniture had taken hold. This house and reworked site, in addition to meeting a very specific program, are *about* these interests, as well as the place's history.

To the barn, which was fully rebuilt along its original lines, was appended a silo-shaped addition. A Modern Bay Regional garage fronts the street, and a path to the cabin and cottage is oriented to handsome views of the Bay. Inside, under carefully worked wooden trusses and ceiling, a long room opens to the view and offers a setting for Modern furniture. Below, the kitchen, whose walls are fashioned from polychrome Mexican tile, faces a serene, Japanese-inspired garden. The adjacent bedroom is reached through a long, skylit study/gallery, whose glass floor admits light to the story below. This room is topped by a shallow, apparently hovering, Modern-inspired white vault.

While architectural histories, design monthlies, and various big thinkers seek the clear statement, the rich possibilities of the *apropos* mixed message are worth remembering. In the pages of *Architectural Digest*, what would sustain the interests of Hadrian?

1. Garage
2. Cottage
3. Gallery
4. Master Bedroom
5. Kitchen
6. Study
7. Guest Bedroom
8. Dining
9. Living

Lower Level Plan

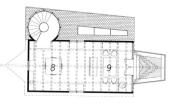

Upper Level Plan

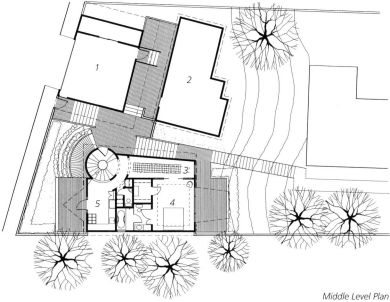

Middle Level Plan

Left: *Top floor trellised wood deck extends toward view of downtown San Francisco.*

Opposite Page: *Cantilevered deck is positioned among treetops.*

Following Spread: *Silo-shaped tower was added to the existing gambrel roofed "barn."*

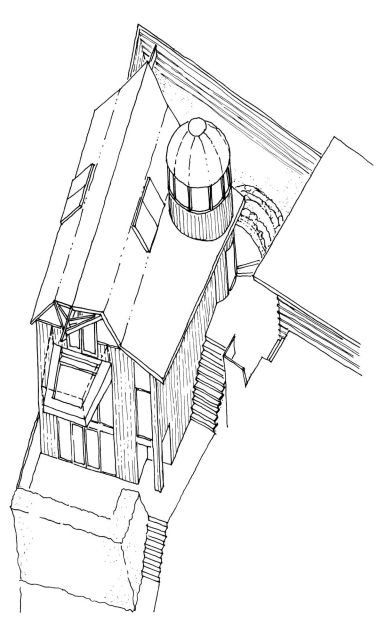

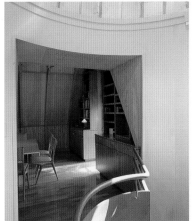

Left: *Top floor is contained within barn's gambrel roof.*

Opposite Page: *Including living and dining, long room on top floor is finished in exposed cedar framing and plywood. Stained glass panel created by the client's daughter.*

Following Spread Left: *Views from, toward stair tower.* **Right:** *Downtown San Francisco appears through cypress and pine trees.*

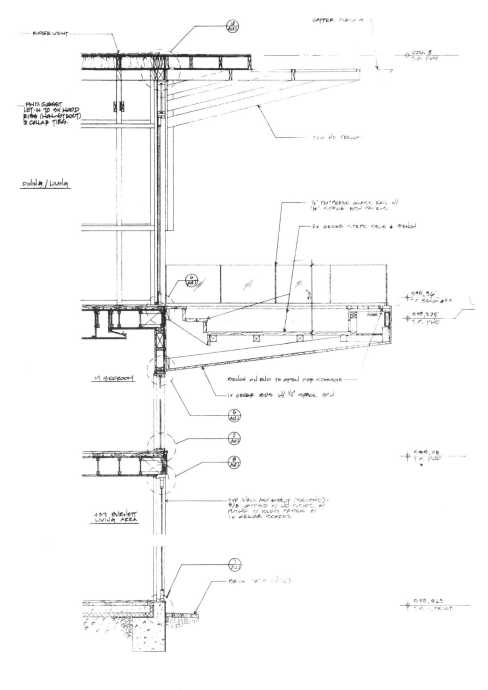

WALL SECTION - EAST WALL

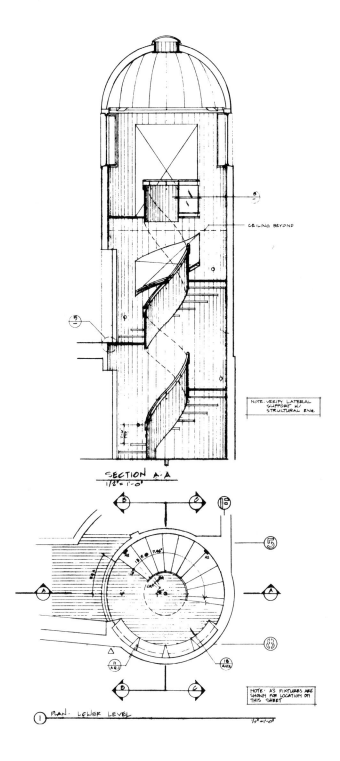

SECTION A-A
1/2" = 1'-0"

CEILING BEYOND

NOTE: VERIFY LATERAL SUPPORT W/ STRUCTURAL ENG.

NOTE: A3 FIXTURES ARE SHOWN FOR LOCATION ON THIS SHEET

① PLAN: LOWER LEVEL

1/2" = 1'-0"

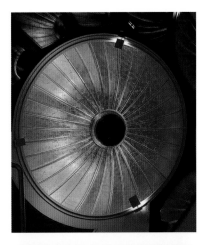

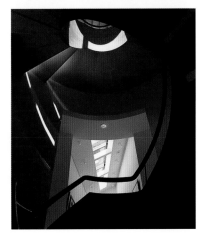

Left: *Gold-finished circular stair, contained in cedar board finished tower, spirals to its apogee beneath a glittering prefabricated silo dome.*

Opposite Page: *Circular stair support and rail, torch-cut from a single piece of steel pipe, is patented by the architects.*

Right: Views between kitchen and stair tower.

Opposite Page: Kitchen is finished in random-patterned Mexican ceramic tiles, color-stained wood panels, and stainless steel.

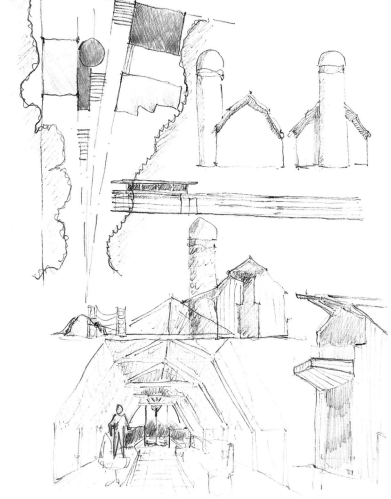

Right: Walls of shower/bath are 12-inch (30-cm) square translucent glass tiles. Ceiling and tub face are 1-inch (2.5-cm) square glass mosaic tiles.

Opposite Page Above: Ceiling of bedroom is a suspended arc, lit behind its edges.
Below: Entrance to sauna leads from not-quite-random-patterned ceramic tile bath.

Key Notes

1. 12" x 12" Glass tile.
2. Tile #2.
3. Mirror, flush with tile.
4. Wood cabinet, stained. R out out face 1/4" to align with every other tile.
5. Wood cabinet, stained with 1" onyx counter.
6. Glass holder.
7. Toothbrush holder.
8. Towel bar.
9. Towel shelf.
10. Grab bar.
11. Glass shower enclosure
12. Recessed, mirrored, medicine cabinet with no frame. Wrap in gyp board to maintain one-hour fire rating in wall.
13. Toilet paper holder.
14. Recessed wood cabinet, stained.
15. Towel hooks.
16. Tub controls.
17. Shower control.
18. Tile seat.
19. Laundry hamper.
20. Light fixture.
20. Custom acrylic light fixture, wet location.

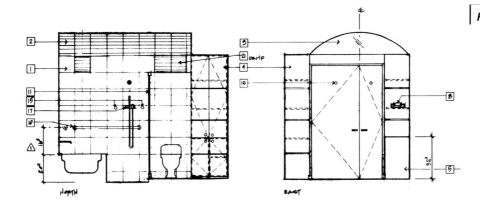

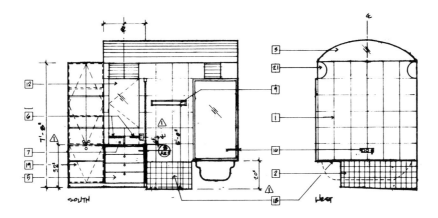

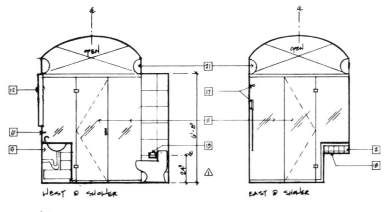

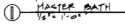

MASTER BATH
1/2" = 1'-0"

Roth Residence
Oakland, California

In the turbulent aftermath of catastrophe, it is something like human instinct to try to restore the calm born of familiarity—to not only pick up the pieces, but arrange them just as they had been before. Immediately in the wake of the 1991 Oakland Hills firestorm that destroyed upwards of three thousand dwellings, survivors expressed their intentions to reconstruct, exactly, what had been lost.

In the intervening years, of course, very little has been put back as it was. Interests and tastes change. Memories, even of catastrophe, fade. This, too, is part of human nature.

One neglected truth about the East Bay hills is that calamitous wildfires are dependably recurrent phenomena. An 1896 fire in nearby Berkeley incinerated scores of houses; and a 1923 fire in much the same area destroyed hundreds more.

This later fire had a profound effect on building practices in the hills, seen especially vividly in houses designed by Bernard Maybeck, who, after 1923, eschewed wood siding, trellises, and shingles in favor of stucco and concrete. The 1991 firestorm, of course, devoured wood and stucco-clad houses of all ages with equal ardor. After this, new regulations concerning materials, landscaping, and building assemblies have been offered, with the idea of preventing yet another large-scale fire. We'll see.

Rather than forgetting history, and without relishing catastrophe, this house is about the 1991 and earlier fires, as well as the place's first inhabitant. The largely level site possesses a glorious prospect of San Francisco Bay. An appealing 1920s Chalet style Arts and Crafts bungalow had stood on the site but had burned to its foundation in the recent fire. The client, whose nearby house had also burned, came to an early meeting with his sketch of a courtyard dwelling oriented toward the view.

This 3,000-square-foot (280-square-meter) house is organized in three blocks set around a courtyard whose open side faces the Bay. In addition to their domestic purposes, these blocks stand for the recurring pattern of building, inhabiting, and calamity in the Oakland Hills.

The street-fronting block, stucco and timber with wide overhanging eaves, formally resembles the Chalet Style predecessor. The library tower, clad in blackened copper shingles, recalls the charred monolithic chimneys that were new, if temporary, landmarks after the fire. Across the courtyard, the third block, with its exoskeleton of wood framing members and plywood, appears to be under construction.

A red sandstone courtyard is crisscrossed by the concrete foundations of the earlier house and provides for life out-of-doors. From the court's heart springs a long, narrow water channel, extending towards the Bay and reflecting it. This is a still, even serene, spot, made not of the calm said to precede a storm, but of that which runs in its wake.

1. *Living Room*
2. *Entry*
3. *Kitchen*
4. *Dining*
5. *Bedroom*
6. *Master Bedroom*
7. *Library*

Second Level Plan

First Level Plan

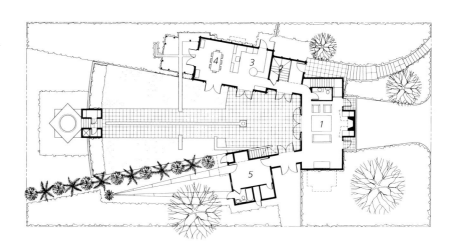

Left: The open side of the courtyard faces a view toward the Bay and San Francisco beyond. A narrow trough, a runnel, carries water toward a spa at the property's edge.

Opposite Page: One of the house's blocks, its framing exposed, and, it seems, in the process of construction. It is fashioned in stained cedar boards and plywood.

Following Spread: House's three blocks are finished in cedar plywood and lumber; integrally colored stucco; and copper-faced shingles.

Right: *Neighbors-like the client, survivors of the Oakland Hills firestorm-claim to see, in the house's street-facing block, the form of a phoenix rising.*

Opposite Page Above: *Cedar framing, "under construction," provides the exoskeleton of an outdoor room.* **Below:** *Seared concrete foundations from the pre-Firestorm house are preserved in the landscape.*

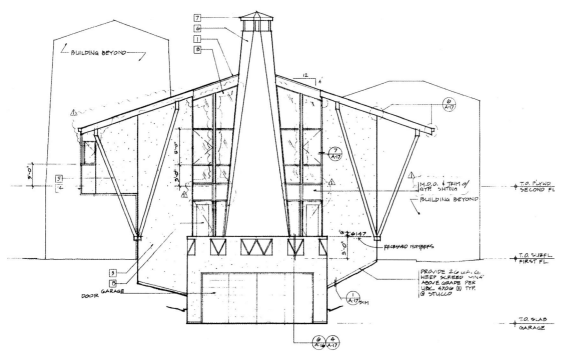

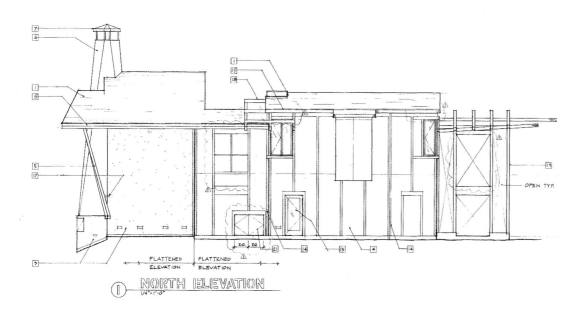

② **EAST ELEVATION**
1/4"=1'-0"

BUILDING BEYOND

12

⑥
A·17

⑦
A·17

M.D.O. & TRM o/
GYP. SHTING
BUILDING BEYOND

T.O. PLYWD
SECOND FL.

3·0"

5·0"

RECESSED NUMBERS

T.O. SUBFL.
FIRST FL.

PROVIDE 26 GA. G.
WEEP SCREED MIN 4"
ABOVE GRADE PER
UBC 4706 (B) TYP.
@ STUCCO

3·0"

DOOR   GARAGE

T.O. SLAB
GARAGE

⑥   ④
A·16 A·17

① **NORTH ELEVATION**
1/4"=1'-0"

FLATTENED
ELEVATION

FLATTENED
ELEVATION

OPEN TYP.

EQ   EQ

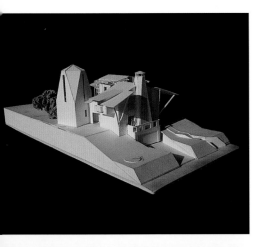

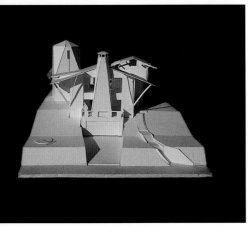

Left: Library/guest bedroom block, clad in copper-faced asphalt shingles, resembles the masonry chimneys that were the most prominent landmarks of the post-Firestorm landscape.

Opposite Page: Study model.

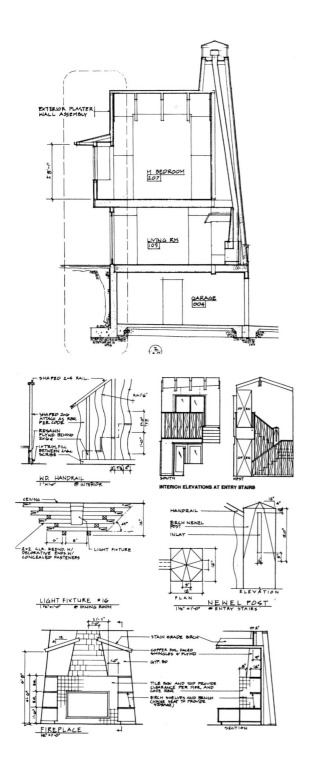

Left Top: *Fireplace is finished in metallic copper ceramic tiles.* **Center:** *Stair rail, patterned on California Mission woodwork, is made of Douglas Fir.* **Bottom:** *Bathroom counter and sink are underlit Mexican onyx and glass.*

Opposite Page: *Fireplace inglenook is a miniature of the house's street-facing elevation.*

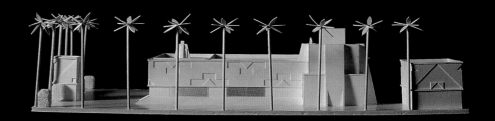
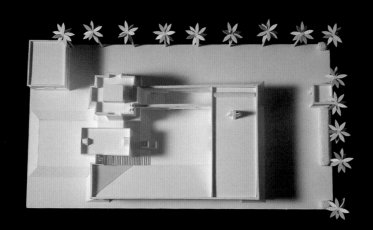
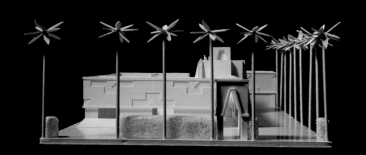
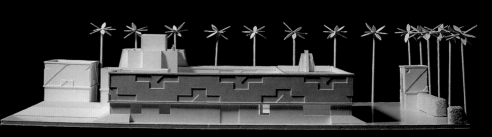

Saravia Residence
Tegucigalpa, Honduras

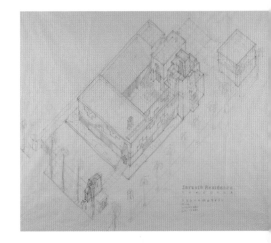

The contractor who assembled the wood framing for both the Allen Residence and Six Houses project asked that we design a new house for his extended family and himself, in a residential development adjacent to a golf course in the suburbs of the capitol of Honduras. He sought a moderately-sized dwelling, set about a court, with public rooms closer to the street and private areas towards the links.

The environs of Tegucigalpa must surely be at the frontier of this form of residential development, which began in the United States and has since spread globally. Houses adjacent to our client's are turned-out "Spanish," with red clay tile roofs, white stucco walls, and dark woodwork. This aggressively bland style, so characteristic of so much sprawl in so many countries, nonetheless has among its roots vivid and memorable places, including Los Angeles in the 1920s, Mexico in the seventeenth and eighteenth centuries, and Spain in the centuries preceding. Over time, style may be thought to travel.

Another appealing, if minor, expression of 1920s Los Angeleno interest in exotic places was the Mayan Revival, which saw stores, gas stations, and especially houses made up as small-scale temples and observatories, often set in lush, though tiny, jungles. Whetting the appetite for this variety of architectural scenography, no doubt, were the images of vine-entangled Central American cities uncovered in the late nineteenth and early twentieth centuries, as well as Hollywood productions and stage revues like "The Court of Montezuma."

Of course, the most prolific revivers of the Mayan style were the Maya, who recombined and reiterated the mode's characteristic forms over six centuries. With the proximity of Copan and other archaeological sites to the lot by the golf course, we thought it time to revive the Mayan Revival, to bring home a wayward style that had earlier wandered to Los Angeles. Entrance to the house is through a patterned street-fronting gate, set on axis with an open, skylit corridor leading

Above: House is screened on two sides by lines of tall palms.

Opposite Page: Saravia Residence includes Mayan Revival motifs and architectural devices, including a wide patterned frieze forming the tops of walls.

Following Spread Left: House is sited about a rectangular courtyard and is single-storied toward the street, while rising to three stories at one corner. *Right:* At the street, a gate whose opening is the characteristic form of a Mayan vault begins a procession to the house, courtyard, and stepped temple forms rising beyond.

to the public rooms and, beyond, to the court. The house appears set on a stone plinth, above which a plain, horizontal band is topped by a vigorously geometrically textured wall. Rooms and circulation open to a large court at the house's center, from which are stairs to the roof. A stepped tower at the court's corner houses the owners' rooms and provides a high platform with views to the dense forest in the distance and aspiring Tiger Woodses closer by.

Lanscaping at the house's perimeter is lush, including tall palms as well as deep green, fast-growing, invasive vines and shrubs pulling at the place's walls. At the court, architectural forms rest on a luxuriant grass carpet, as is the current custom at archaeological sites.

With architectural style, history repeats itself less as tragedy or farce than as romance, sentimental and "trashy" as often as not, attending to the contemporary possibilities of places with evocative, if imagined, pasts.

1. Living
2. Dining
3. Kitchen
4. Family Room
5. Bedroom
6. Garage
7. Study
8. Open to Below
9. Roof Deck
10. Terrace

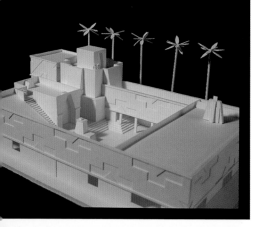

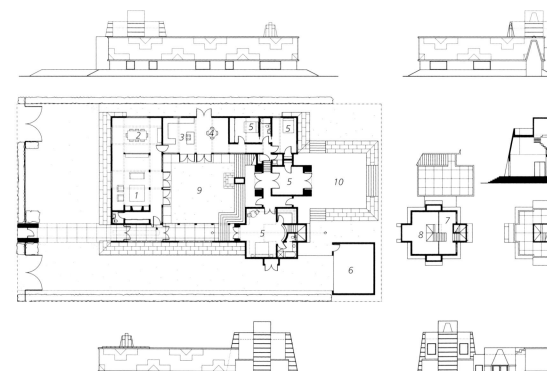

Plan, elevations, and sections

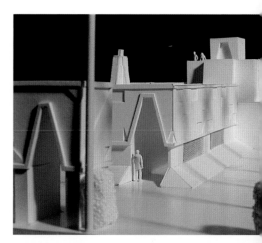

Six Houses

Oakland, California

The design of houses often begins considering their contexts—the ways landscape, topography, climate, and orientation bear on a site, for example; the character and arrangements of adjacent (or distant) buildings; clients' purposes and capacities; the place's social circumstances and its history; as well as codes, building practices, etc. From this singular welter, the architect prays, schemes emerge.

Of course, there are more contexts than even these, including the designers' backgrounds and enthusiasms. Bruce Goff remarked on this, noting, "In architecture there's the reason you do something, and then there's the real reason." His flamboyantly eccentric *oeuvre*, especially the houses, is testimony to the force of the "real reason."

Many of the most memorable and exciting houses seem born of especially felicitous contexts. With Fallingwater, Wright employed a rich amalgam of the site's inherent and invented dramas; his clients', the Kaufmanns, interests, as well as their patience and resources; and his own talents and current passions. (To those who doubt clients' capacities for patience, consider that the Kaufmanns kept two sets of dining room furniture—the chairs and table they actually used, and the FLW-designed set they pulled out when Frank came calling.)

Of course, in the absence of fully felicitous contexts, it is often necessary to make do. A local lefty radio station concludes its daily current affairs broadcast with the exhortation "If you don't like the news, go out and make some of your own." Right on. With these three pairs of modestly sized speculative houses (the first pair is complete, the second just finishing up), set in a dark eucalyptus forest along a busy street in the Oakland Hills, outside any established neighborhood—and with our client a very shallow-pocketed developer—we sought an outsized architectural conceit. If the existing contexts were unsuggestive, we thought to invent new ones. Right on.

Each house, though planned as part of mirror-image pairs, is imagined as a discrete example of Spanish-influenced building in California, from the eighteenth century through to the twenty-first. Houses are styled Mission, Monterey Colonial, Victorian, Art Deco, Modern, as well as Deconstructivist Spanish, which we thought broke new ground. If they are not arranged chronologically, the past is seldom so tidy.

The familiar "Spanish-y" palette of materials (plaster, clay roof tiles, and patterned ceramic tilework, painted metalwork) is employed throughout, but against the panoply of historical forms and in a range of hues and finishes. A popular 1960s cartoon pictures a confused-looking man, returning from work, unable to pick out his house from its suburban Ranch style neighbors. If the hard-nosed economic and social contexts of tract building continue to augur for the nearly seamless nowhere of much of suburbia, we hope this brightly-hued, bougainvillea-bedecked conceit makes it easier to find one's way home.

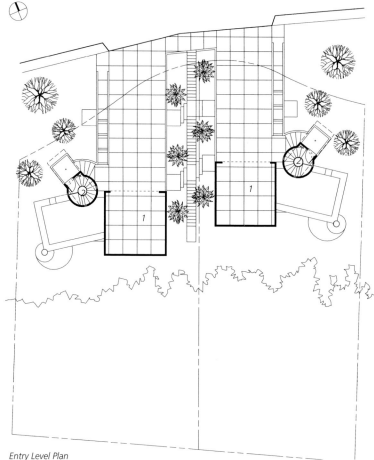

1. Garage
2. Entry Deck
3. Master Bedroom
4. Master Bathroom
5. Study
6. Closet
7. Kitchen
8. Dining Room
9. Living Room
10. Family Room
11. Bedroom
12. Deck

Lower Level Plan

Entry Level Plan

Upper Level Plan

Left: *Compact rooms are high-ceilinged, with ceramic tile floors, and gleaming circular stairs.*

Opposite Page: *Stairs from Skyline Boulevard lead to balcony at entry/stair tower, overlooking garden below.*

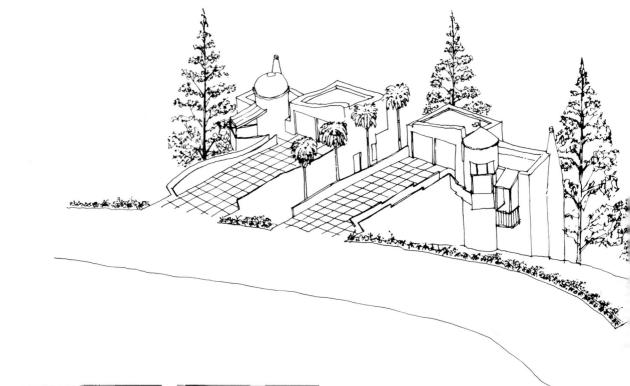

Right: House's exteriors are in a variety of hues of integrally colored stucco.

Opposite Page: Construction photographs.

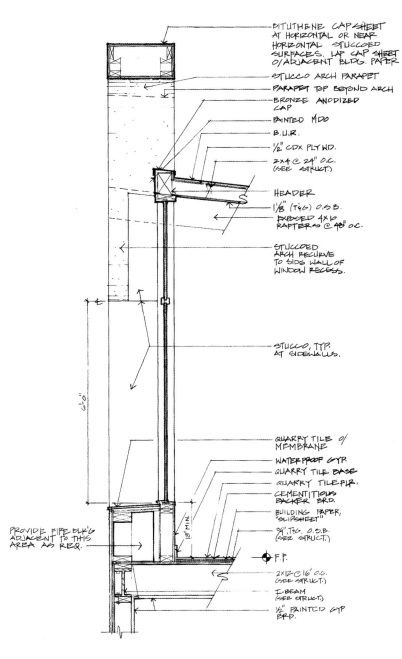

BITUTHENE CAP SHEET AT HORIZONTAL OR NEAR HORIZONTAL STUCCOED SURFACES. LAP CAP SHEET O/ADJACENT BLDG. PAPER

STUCCO ARCH PARAPET

PARAPET TOP BEYOND ARCH

BRONZE ANODIZED CAP

PAINTED MDO

B.U.R.

½" CDX PLY WD.

2x4 @ 24" O.C. (SEE STRUCT.)

HEADER

1⅛" (T&G) O.S.B.

EXPOSED 4x10 RAFTERS @ 48" O.C.

STUCCOED ARCH RECURVE TO SIDE WALL OF WINDOW RECESS.

STUCCO, TYP. AT SIDEWALLS.

6'-0"

QUARRY TILE O/ MEMBRANE

WATERPROOF GYP.

QUARRY TILE BASE

QUARRY TILE FLR.

CEMENTITIOUS BACKER BRD.

BUILDING PAPER, "SLIPSHEET"

¾" T&G O.S.B. (SEE STRUCT.)

18" MIN.

F.F.

PROVIDE FIRE BLK'G ADJACENT TO THIS AREA AS REQ.

2x12 @ 16" O.C. (SEE STRUCT.)

I-BEAM (SEE STRUCT.)

½" PAINTED GYP BRD.

WALL SECTION @ LIVING ROOM WINDOW
SCALE ¾" = 1'-0"

Left Above: Simple, tall rooms are daylit on two sides. **Middle:** Front door includes oversized, decorative hinges, whose scroll-shaped form is shared by the tower's circular stairs. **Below:** Circular stairs, patented by architects, spiral to floors below.

Opposite Page: Outsized balcony at entry/stair tower.

Selected Buildings and Projects

Jordan Residence
Oakland, CA

Project Staff: Joel Miroglio
Lot Size: 5,000 sf/460 sm
Building Size: 1,400 sf/130 sm
Date of Design: 1992
Construction Completed: 1993

Roth Residence
Oakland, CA

Project Staff: John Cooley,
Jarrell Connor
Lot Size: 12,000 sf/1,110 sm
Building Size: 3,600 sf/330 sm
Date of Design: 1995
Construction Completed: 1996

Telegraph Hill House
San Francisco, CA

Project Staff: Scott Glendinning,
Judy Choi
Lot Size: 1,200 sf/110 sm
Building Size: 1,100 sf/100 sm lower unit,
2,200 sf/200 sm upper unit
Date of Design: 1984
Construction Completed: 1986

Rancho Diablo
Lafayette, CA

Project Staff: Alec Iacono, Michelle
Steed, Andrew Woolman
Lot Size: 20 acres/8 hectares
Building Size: 2,300 sf/210 sm renovation,
3,700 sf/340 sm addition in process
Date of Design: 1989 renovation,
1997 addition, 1998 addition
Construction Completed: 1933
original, 1989 renovation

Allen Residence
Oakland, CA

Project Staff: Greg Taylor, John Cooley
Lot Size: 8,600 sf/800 sm
Building Size: 3,100 sf/290 sm
Date of Design: 1993
Construction Completed: 1994

Saravia Residence
Tegucigalpa, Honduras

Project Staff: Alec Iacono
Lot Size: 15,000 sf/1,400 sm
Building Size: 3,500 sf/325 sm
Date of Design: 1997
Date to be completed: 2000

Querio Residence
Oakland, CA

Project Staff: Keith Rivera,
Rosanna Javier
Lot Size: 2,700 sf/250 sm
Building Size: 5,000 sf/460 sm
Date of Design: 1985
Construction Completed: 1988

Tabancay/Austin Residence
Berkeley, CA

Project Staff: Kriss Raupach,
Carrie Kingman
Lot Size: 6,250 sf/580 sm
Building Size: 4,000 sf/370 sm
Date of Design: 1990
Construction Completed: 1991

House on Twin Peaks
San Francisco, CA

Project Staff: Greg Taylor, Christina
Francavillese, and Kriss Raupach
Lot Size: 10,000 sf/930 sm
Building Size: 2,600 sf/240 sm
Date of Design: 1994
Construction Completed: 1996

6 Houses
Oakland, CA

Project Staff: Alec Iacono
Lot Size: 2 sites, 6,000 sf/560 sm each
Building Size: 2 sites, 2,300 sf/210 sm each
Date of Design: 1997
Construction Completed: 2000

Described in *Vanity Fair* as "the court jester of California architecture," Ace Architects has authored more than three hundred highly idiosyncratic buildings and interiors over the past 20 years. Often exuberant, spatially charged, and vividly polychromatic, as well as flat-out fun, Ace places are the antithesis of the current vogue for cool, minimal, abstract, and modern.

In an age favoring architectural specialization, Ace's work could scarcely be more various. Consider their projects—theme parks, office buildings, commercial districts; houses, playhouses, doghouses, and children's building blocks. Their client list includes Walt Disney's Imagineers, World Savings, the University of California, and the Archive of Love, O-Town Beauty, and Mercado Guadalajara #2. Ace Architects has designed buildings styled Gothic, Mayan, and Japanese as well as structures resembling sea monsters, hot dogs, and the flame-colored flower of the exotic monkeyhand tree.

There is variety, too, in the coverage of the firm's work—the *New York Times* and *Architectural Digest*, as well as the *Magic Leaf* and *East Bay Express*. Perhaps not surprisingly, Ace Architects' work is more often noticed in the popular than in the American professional press. A story suggestion to *Progressive Architecture* from Ace's photographer brought this response—"The project looks like a lot of fun. It didn't raise much interest here." *Progressive Architecture* has since folded; Ace continues to work. Just as unsurprisingly, the foreign architectural press is much interested in Ace, and projects have been featured in journals in England, Germany, Italy, Japan, Spain, Turkey, the United Arab Emirates, even the former Yugoslavia. The work has, as well, inspired criticism; this, too, has taken many forms. The blood of architecture critics has boiled, and television anchors have fumed and seethed. Ace receives anonymous letters and telephone calls. Its buildings are marked with erudite, art-critical graffiti. A Berkeley city planning commissioner dressed, one Halloween, as the firm's latest building in that city. It was, he said, the most frightening costume he could imagine. Other criticism has been less genteel, though equally emphatic. The contractor's punch list for an almost-completed commercial building in San Jose, California included the repair of several small-caliber bullet holes.

What provokes such, well, deeply felt responses? Ace believes that architecture, like all the arts, is capable of pursuing the universe of subject matter, from sea monsters to monkeyhand flowers. The most usual of architectural subjects is, of course, architecture; consequently, it is no surprise that what most buildings most resemble is other buildings. Ace's interests range wider, and their architecture is not necessarily only architectural. Too, rather than disguise its enthusiasm beneath layers of abstraction, Ace renders the subjects (these are always multiple) of its buildings vividly, unmistakably, representationally. A sea monster's eyes glow red, its scales are green, its beak angular and sharp.

Ace has received a range of architectural distinctions, including awards from the Graham Foundation, American Institute of Architects, and California Preservation Foundation. The firm has twice been included with *Architectural Digest*'s "AD 100."

Photographic Credits

Russell Abraham

Steven Brooks

Alec Iacono

Christopher Irion

Environmental Design Archive, UC Berkeley

Jennifer Levy

Alan Weintraub

Acknowledgments

Ace Architects Staff

Susan Evans

Alec Iacono

Residential Clients

John Allen

Evelyn and Bob Apte

Lise and Neal Blumenfeld

Dixie Jordan

Jennifer Kenny and Roberto Reichard

Mimi Querio

David Roth

Mario Saravia

Norma and Bruce Siegel

Ruth Tabancay and Mick Austin

Evelyn Topper

Rockport Publishers

Don Fluckinger

Rosalie Grattaroti

Danielle Lavallee

Oscar Riera Ojeda

Winnie Prentiss